HOW
STARBUCKS
CHANGED
THE WORLD

HOW
STARBUCKS
CHANGED
THE WORLD

MARIE BUSSING-BURKS

JAICO PUBLISHING HOUSE

Ahmedabad Bangalore Bhopal Chennai
Delhi Hyderabad Kolkata Lucknow Mumbai

Published by Jaico Publishing House
A-2 Jash Chambers, 7-A Sir Phirozshah Mehta Road
Fort, Mumbai - 400 001
jaicopub@jaicobooks.com
www.jaicobooks.com

Originally published in hard cover by Greenwood Press,
an imprint of ABC-CLIO, LLC
Santa Barbara, CA

Published in arrangement with
ABC-CLIO, LLC, Santa Barbara, CA
All rights reserved

HOW STARBUCKS CHANGED THE WORLD
ISBN 978-81-8495-128-8

First Jaico Impression: 2010

Printed by
Rashmi Graphics
#3, Amrutwel CHS Ltd., C.S. #50/74
Ganesh Galli, Lalbaug, Mumbai-400 012
E-mail: tiwarijp@vsnl.net

Dedicated to my wonderful friends:
Lee Ann, Mary Beth, Susan,
Anne, Caren, Jan, Deb, and Sara

Contents

Contents

Acknowledgments

I would like to thank Jeff Olson, senior acquisitions editor at ABC-CLIO/
Greenwood Press, for allowing me this exciting opportunity to explore the
past, current, and transitioning business practices of Starbucks. It has been
a magnificent learning experience uncovering how the one-store coffee retailer grew to be a global coffee company with over 16,000 stores. It is my
pleasure to be able to share knowledge about this premium coffee retailer
and top-notch corporate business with young adult readers.

My sincere gratitude is also extended to Cathy Bowman for her excellent editorial assistance. It is greatly appreciated and valued.

A group of highly skilled professionals in the fields of coffee, philanthropy, and business shared their time and expertise in the development
of this book. I owe a debt of gratitude to Katie Barrow, public relations
manager, TransFair USA; Shari Berenbach, president and CEO, Calvert
Foundation; James Cleveland, president, Jumpstart; Ted Lingle, executive
director, Coffee Quality Institute; and a spokesperson from the ICE Futures
U.S. The input from these experts added significantly to depth of the text
and my understanding of Starbucks Corporation. A note of appreciation
is also given to the Starbucks cafes in my hometown of Evansville, Indiana,
for providing superb coffee and inspiration for my writing.

Lastly, my thanks go to my husband, Barry; my children, Amie and
Katie; my mother, Connie; my brother, Bill; my sister-in-law, Phyllis; and
my in-laws, Basil and Iris, who always encourage my writing. And a
special thank-you to my aunt, Marilyn Stone, who was quick to send
me current clippings and updates from the news media on Starbucks'
fast-paced activities.

Introduction

Is not the very name, COFFEE, suggestive of aromatic odors?
—Robert Hewitt, Jr., *Coffee: Its History, Cultivation, and Uses* (1872)

Java, cup of joe, bean juice, mocha, or just plain coffee—whatever you call it, this beverage conjures up feelings of comfort, warmth, and kinship. A morning eye-opening ritual for many, pots of this black beverage brew in homes, offices, restaurants, and, of course, the coffeehouse throughout the day. As the world's largest consumers, Americans drink more than 300 million cups of coffee each day.

Coffee Talk

Coffee is the world's second most traded commodity. Do you know the first?

You guessed it—oil.

How did this steaming roasted bean come to permeate our lives and culture? The story of coffee dates back more than one thousand years. It has swept the globe, only to explode in Seattle, Washington, now the symbolic Coffee Capital of the World. The coffee tree is native to Ethiopia. In fact, the name *coffee* is thought to be a derivation of Kaffa, an Ethiopian province.

A popular legend maintains the origin of coffee can be traced to a simple Ethiopian goat herder named Kaldi. One day while tending the flock, Kaldi observed his goats dancing. They had been eating bright red coffee berries, and, out of curiosity, Kaldi chewed a few himself. He discovered the invigorating effects of the beans and soon began dancing with his goats.

Kaldi shared the story of the special berries with a monk from a nearby monastery. The monk threw the berries onto an open fire, suspecting evil. A wonderful aroma filled the air, and the holy man changed his

Berries after harvesting.

mind, scooping the beans from the fire to make a watery beverage with
the powder. Hence, the first cup of coffee. The monk and his fellows drank
the substance in order to stay awake during their all-night religious cer-
emonies.

It is known that East African tribes would mix ground coffee beans
into a paste with animal fat. This mixture provided energy to their war-
riors and was a primitive version of today's power bars.

Coffee was taken from Ethiopia to the Yemen province of Arabia in
the 15th century. Serious cultivation of the trees began at that time by
the Yemenis, long famous as the world's suppliers of coffee. The Arabs
guarded their monopoly on coffee and made exportation of coffee plants
illegal so the crop could not be grown elsewhere. Before coffee beans could
be sold, they were boiled to make them infertile. The coffee bean trade was
first centered in the Yemeni port of Mocha and then expanded to Mecca,
the most important trading center of the world, to Turkey, and to Egypt.
Coffee's popularity became widespread throughout the Islamic world. In
fact, the first coffeehouses were opened in Mecca and called *kaveh kanes*.
It was against the Muslim faith to drink wine or other alcoholic spirits, so
coffee became a favored alternative. Coffeehouses quickly spread throughout the Middle East during the 15th century as places where men would
gather to drink coffee, sing, tell stories, listen to music, and play chess.

Although banned in subsequent periods of history for its role in political controversy, the coffeehouse was an integral part of Islamic culture during this time.

The Dutch were the first to carry a live coffee seedling out of Yemen, transporting it to Holland in 1616. There, the seedlings were grown in greenhouses. The Dutch began cultivating large-scale plantations in their colonies in Indonesia, on the islands of Java, Sumatra, Sulawesi, and Bali. Soon, the Dutch colonies were the main suppliers of coffee for all of Europe. Coffee was widespread in Europe by the mid-17th century, especially in England, France, and Holland.

In 1720, a French naval officer named Gabriel Mathieu de Clieu, serving on the Caribbean island of Martinique, acquired a coffee seedling while in Paris on leave. His goal was to get the tree back to Martinique safely, but a threat from pirates, a terrible storm, and even a jealous fight over the coffee plant all marked the ship's journey. When drinking water was rationed, de Clieu unselfishly gave up most of his water ration to keep the coffee plant alive. The plant miraculously survived the trip and thrived in its new environment. By 1777, it is recorded, there were between 18 million and 19 million coffee trees on Martinique.

Meanwhile, coffeehouses were gaining popularity all over Europe as centers of social interaction where people could talk, read, or write in solitude. The first coffeehouse opened in Britain in 1652. The British called their coffeehouses Penny Universities, because that was the price for admittance to the shop where one could drink coffee, read newspapers, and do business. Information exchanged at the coffeehouse was invaluable for businessmen conducting transactions. Business was handled very informally at the time. Notably, in 1668, Edward Lloyd opened a coffee shop that became a center for marine insurance. Lloyd welcomed those interested in overseas trade, such as ships' captains, merchants, and ship owners. Merchants with ships would ask a broker to find wealthy individuals to risk their personal fortune on the ships and cargo. That coffeehouse evolved into the world-renowned Lloyd's of London insurance company, today home to the most experienced specialist underwriters in the world. In England, as in America, the purpose of the early coffeehouse was business.

The first mention of coffee being drunk in North America dates from 1668, and coffeehouses soon followed. The Tontine Coffee House in New York was the original location for the New York Stock Exchange in 1792, because regular business and transactions were conducted there. In the United States, the coffeehouse cultural scene bloomed in the early 1960s. Writers, musicians, and intellectuals used coffeehouses as venues for their work. Often accompanied by guitarists, folk musicians and poets freely expressed thoughts and political leanings in an open atmosphere. The coffeehouse scene thrived in the Pacific Northwest, and Starbucks was soon at the forefront.

On March 29, 1971, Starbucks opened its first store in Seattle, in the Harbor Heights Hotel at Pike Place Market. Starbucks might have begun as one local roaster and retailer, but today, it has transitioned into the largest coffeehouse chain in the world, with more than 16,680 locations in 47 countries. The stores carry a variety of handcrafted beverages, coffee drinks, teas, food items, roasted beans, and coffee accessories.

In less than four decades, Starbucks has earned phenomenal success. It has changed the way people enjoy coffee, so much so that the average Starbucks customer visits a store 18 times each month, and the Starbucks experience is an important part of people's lives. Despite challenges along the way, this success story had a game plan. Let us explore the story of Starbucks, its strategy, and how it became a corporation that changed the world.

Coffee Talk

Coffee is produced in over 60 countries and provides a living for 25 million coffee farmers around the world.

Chapter One

Origins and History of Starbucks

Starbucks didn't invent coffee, of course; it just did something with it that no one thought possible.
—Taylor Clark, *Starbucked: A Double Tall Tale of Caffeine, Commerce, and Culture* (2007)

Before Starbucks, going out for coffee meant a cup of steaming black brew, friendly conversation, and sharing the booths with neighboring breakfast and lunch customers. But in just a few decades, Starbucks would completely change the American coffee scene. High-priced brews, lattes, Frappuccinos, and espressos awaken the senses of the 50 million customers it serves every week around the world. Touting more than 30 blends and single-origin coffees, Starbucks has more than 87,000 customizable drink combinations when you consider the fine details of milk add-ins, shots, syrups, and whips.

Three Seattle friends started the company—Gordon Bowker, Jerry Baldwin, and Zev Siegl. Bowker was a writer, Baldwin was an English teacher, and Siegl was a history teacher. The original name of the first store, opened in 1971, was Starbucks Coffee, Tea, and Spices. Later, the name was changed to Starbucks Coffee Company. Starbucks' original logo was a chocolate brown, bare-breasted mermaid siren with long hair, encircled by the company name. Today's contemporary green logo sports a more updated and modest mermaid.

Starbucks was named after Starbuck, first mate of the whaleship *Pequod* in Herman Melville's *Moby Dick*. Terry Heckler, with whom Bowker had an ad agency, had looked at an old mining map of the Cascades and Mount Rainer one day, spotting a town called Starbo. The name Starbo reminded Bowker of the first mate in *Moby Dick,* Starbuck. The character had nothing to do with coffee; Bowker just liked how the sound of the word "popped." Starbuck was pluralized for ease of use and was approved by the trio.

The friends were not skilled in the coffee business. At the time, all they knew was that a good cup of coffee was hard to find. One day over lunch,

Bowker was discussing the beans he had purchased on one of his monthly trips to Vancouver, British Columbia, to purchase coffee. That was the nearest place he could get a decent cup of coffee. They all preferred coffee from dark-roasted arabica beans, rather than the lower-quality, less-flavorful robusta beans more commonly used. Tired of importing his own beans on his monthly runs to Canada, Bowker and his two friends dreamed up the scheme of selling coffee in Seattle, and Starbucks was born.

THE BEGINNINGS

Bowker, Baldwin, and Siegl knew they needed the right coffee to sell. Siegl went south to California to find the goods. A Dutchman, Alfred Peet, was doing big business from his storefront in Berkeley—Peet's Coffee & Tea. Siegl knocked on his door looking for someone to roast coffee for Starbucks. Peet agreed to supply the fledgling shop with coffee if the founders would each work at his Berkeley shop for a week to train in the coffee business. So, for Starbucks' first year in business, Peet roasted the beans while teaching his entrepreneurial friends. Bowker, Baldwin, and Siegl visited Peet's many times to learn about quality coffee and proper roasting techniques from this master.

According to Taylor Clark, the three invested $1,350 each and together borrowed $5,000 from the bank. Rent on the first store was just $137 a month (*Starbucked: A Double Tall Tale of Caffeine,* Commerce and Culture 2007, 41–42). Overhead costs were low. Initially, Starbucks did not even sell fresh-brewed coffee by the cup, though samples were available for drinking from porcelain cups. The original purpose of the store was to sell gourmet coffee beans, along with coffee-related merchandise and equipment.

At the start, Siegl was the only paid employee at Starbucks. He wore an apron, scooped the coffee beans, connected with his customers, and was the retail guru. During the first year, Starbucks ordered its coffee beans from Peet's. But when the Seattle shop started moving significant amounts of coffee, Peet could not keep up with the demand, and the partners had to come up with a new plan. They purchased a used coffee roaster from Holland, set up roasting operations, and began experimenting with blends and flavors on their own. Bowker and Baldwin tinkered with Peet's roasting procedures, creating their own unique blends. Baldwin became an accomplished roaster, and Bowker was the marketing genius.

That Starbucks was born and survived the early 1970s in Seattle is a feat in and of itself. Boeing, a major aerospace and defense corporation, was then headquartered there. (In 2001, Boeing moved its headquarters to Chicago, but production remains in Seattle.) The city's largest employer, Boeing went into a major economic downturn just as Starbucks was getting started, due to a national aviation recession. That was topped off by Congress withdrawing funding for the production of an American supersonic transport Boeing had developed. The company cut its workforce from

The first Starbucks was opened in Pike Place Market in Seattle, Washington, on March 30, 1971.

80,400 in early 1970 to 37,200 by October 1971. Many people, unable to find work in the area, were forced to move away. The situation was so extreme that two real estate agents, with a hint of humor, put up a billboard on the city's outskirts that read, "Will the last person leaving Seattle—turn out the lights?" However, Seattle did recover after the Boeing crash, and Starbucks coffee sales helped stimulate the local economic recovery.

The first Starbucks store was located in a storefront at the Harbor Heights Hotel at Pike Place Market, where it remained from 1971 to 1976. The flagship store then moved to 1912 Pike Place in Pike Place Market, where it remains today. It was a rustic store, small, with a nautical theme. With the entrepreneurial talents of Baldwin, Bowker, and Siegl, Starbucks slowly grew. A second store opened in the city in 1972. Ten years later, in 1981, Starbucks had a roasting plant and four Seattle retail stores selling whole-bean coffee. Although the company was profitable, in 1980, Siegl decided he wanted to leave Starbucks and pursue other interests. He sold out that year. He felt Starbucks had grown too large and he was more effective in smaller businesses. The roles of the remaining duo shifted, as Baldwin served as president and took over daily operations. Bowker, although still involved with Starbucks, also had outside interests—writing and other entrepreneurial adventures.

Starbucks use the Bing Sutt design in Hong Kong.

THE NEW PLAYER

One of the items found on Starbucks' shelves was the Hammarplast coffeemaker. Hammarplast sold Swedish-designed kitchen equipment and housewares. In 1981, an executive at Hammarplast became curious about why a small retailer in Seattle was ordering large quantities of the company's thermos-type drip coffeemakers. Upon traveling to the Starbucks flagship store in Pike Place Market, Howard Schultz discovered a shop that sold only whole-bean coffee and coffee merchandise and equipment, including Hammarplast coffeemakers in red, yellow, and black. He was instantly intrigued and enamored with the promise he saw in this small retailer. During the next year, the New York-based housewares executive applied and was hired as Starbucks' director of retail operations and marketing. Schultz took a steep pay cut, but in addition to his salary, he was given a small equity share in the business—a share of the company's future. The destiny of Starbucks was changed forever.

In the spring of 1983, Schultz attended an international housewares show in Milan. He was impressed with the Milan espresso bars and the whole Italian coffee bar culture, offering community, camaraderie, and artfully prepared coffee. Starbucks was selling great coffee beans, but it did not serve coffee. Samples were served only in order to give customers a chance to taste the product before buying beans by the pound; but serving coffee and espresso the Italian way, Schultz imagined, could move Starbucks from a great retailer to an experience. He returned to Seattle with a new vision.

When Starbucks opened its sixth store in April 1984, the founders allowed Schultz to test his coffeehouse concept. That store, at the corner of Fourth Avenue and Spring Street in downtown Seattle, was the first Starbucks designed to sell coffee by the pound alongside prepared coffee beverages—regular cups of brewed coffee, as well as the then-unfamiliar espresso drinks so popular in Europe. The response was overwhelming; while a high-performing Starbucks had previously tallied an average daily customer count of 250, within two months, the new store was serving 800 customers a day. The beverage business was definitely a success. But the founders chose not to take the idea of espresso bars any further, deciding rather to concentrate on the business of coffee roasting.

Starbucks, which was majority-owned by Bowker and Baldwin, bought out Peet's Coffee & Tea in 1984. The founders were preoccupied with the acquisition and merging the two companies and were not supportive of the espresso business. Schultz, on the other hand, wanted to open additional stores that would serve coffee and espresso, intent on capturing the warm social interaction he had admired in Italy.

Coffee Talk

Coffee beans retain their peak flavor for only a short period of time. If they haven't sold after eight days, Starbucks donates the coffee beans to food banks.

Convinced the espresso bar concept would be a hit with Americans, Schultz left Starbucks and began his own coffeehouse business. Schultz started the Il Giornale coffee bar chain in 1985. *Il Giornale* is the name of Italy's largest newspaper. *Giornale* means daily; if the company served great coffee, Schultz hoped, customers would come back every day. The coffeehouse sold brewed coffee and espresso beverages. About 30 investors, including Starbucks, which pumped in $150,000, contributed $1.65 million to back the new venture. All beverages were made from Starbucks coffee beans.

On April 6, 1986, the first Italian-style Il Giornale coffeehouse opened. It was a tiny, 700-square-foot store near the main entrance to Seattle's tallest building. Within six months of opening, it was serving 1,000 customers a day.

CHANGE ON THE HORIZON

Bowker and Baldwin eventually became disenchanted with the business development of their start-up. Baldwin wanted to concentrate on the core business of selling quality coffee beans and focused his interests on the Peet's acquisition. Bowker was busy with a variety of business ventures, wanted to do other things, and was pleased to take some cash out of the business. In 1987, Baldwin and Bowker sold the Seattle stores, the roasting plant, and the name Starbucks—keeping only the Peet's assets. In a nearly $4 million deal backed by local investors, Il Giornale acquired the Starbucks assets and changed the unified company's name to Starbucks Corporation. Starbucks was thought to be a catchier and easier-to-pronounce name for Americans than the Italian Il Giornale. Expansion began immediately, aiming toward Schultz's goal to build a national company. Starbucks opened its first locations outside of Seattle in Chicago and Vancouver, British Columbia. By the end of the first fiscal year, Starbucks had 17 stores.

Starbucks was a privately held business from 1987 to 1992. Those years were a critical growth period for the company. Schultz had promised investors in 1987 that Starbucks would open 125 stores in five years. At the end of fiscal 1991, there were 116 stores, all of them in the Northwest or the Chicago area. Starbucks went public on June 26, 1992, at a price of $17 a share, and closed that day at $21.50. Starbucks Corporation's common stock trades on NASDAQ with the ticker symbol SBUX. By the end of fiscal 1992, Schultz had exceeded his goal. There were 165 Starbucks stores. That year, the company expanded to San Francisco, San Diego, Orange County, and Denver.

Since the company went public, the growth has been explosive. At the end of fiscal 2008, there were 16,680 Starbucks stores across the nation and around the world. In 1996, Starbucks went international. The company set the playing field for global growth by opening its first stores in Japan and Singapore, and today, Starbucks is an international brand name, found in more than 47 countries around the world. Its net revenues have reached over $10 billion.

Lest you suppose that Starbucks just sells coffee and coffee beverages, think again: Through the years, Starbucks has gradually added cold, blended beverages; teas; a variety of fresh food; and even a selection of music on compact discs. In addition to its company-operated retail stores, Starbucks now sells coffee through its specialty-group sales and in supermarkets. The company produces a line of bottled coffee beverages and a line of super-premium ice cream through its joint venture partnerships.

YOU DECIDE

Brewing Battle: Arabica versus Robusta Beans

There are two types of coffee beans: *Coffea arabica* (arabica) and *Coffea canephora* (robusta). Starbucks buys only the highest-quality arabica beans in the world and then roasts them to the preferred flavor for each variety. Arabica beans are definitely more expensive, but Starbucks continues to buy only the best arabica coffee it can find. What is the difference?

Arabica coffee accounts for approximately 75 percent of the world's coffee production. It is grown at higher altitudes and thrives in shade. In fact, the higher the altitude, the more flavorful the bean. The taste is more refined, with a milder flavor. Arabica beans can be dark-roasted for a bold, flavorful taste. It is the superior-quality bean and thus carries a premium price.

Robusta, as the name suggests, is a hardier coffee plant and has more resistance to extreme weather conditions. Robusta trees can grow in direct sunlight. When ground and brewed, robusta coffee is known for its high caffeine content and harsh taste. This bean thrives at lower elevations, is easy to grow, and thus is less expensive. Most canned coffee uses the inferior robusta bean, which maximizes profit while minimizing flavor. Robusta beans can't be dark-roasted or they will burn and become bitter.

During the Brazilian frost of 1994, coffee prices skyrocketed. Starbucks executives realized that by purchasing lower-quality robusta beans, the company could maintain its profit margins (the difference between sales and expenses). Even better, they knew that most customers would not notice a blending of high-quality arabica beans with lower-quality robusta. What would you have done—gone for higher profits at the expense of quality? The risk, of course, would be that true coffee aficionados would notice and shun Starbucks, thereby denting the company's theretofore stellar reputation. Or would you have continued to use only the best-quality coffee?

The company remained true to its vision. It was and is dedicated to using only the best-quality beans available—100 percent high-quality arabica beans. Starbucks CEO Schultz concedes that probably fewer than 10 percent of the company's customers would have noticed, yet the leaders chose not to tarnish the Starbucks name.

Chapter Two

The Founders and Early Management Team

For my part, I saw Starbucks not for what it was, but for what it could be.
—Howard Schultz, chairman and CEO of Starbucks,
Pour Your Heart into It (1997)

Starbucks was founded in Seattle in 1971, not by big-business moguls, but by a trio of friends—Gordon Bowker, Jerry Baldwin, and Zev Siegl. All dreamed of sharing their love of high-quality arabica coffee beans with the people of Seattle. By 1981, that dream had grown into four Seattle locations and a strong wholesale business selling coffee to business and restaurant accounts. Yet, little is mentioned or noticed of the original founders today. In fact, when corporate Starbucks celebrated its 30th anniversary in 2001, with reminiscences, coffee, and cake, none of the three was invited. Even so, Starbucks owes much to its founding visionaries, who set out upon a mission to improve people's lives with the aroma and taste of dark-roasted coffee beans.

GORDON BOWKER

The seed of Starbucks can really be attributed to cofounder Gordon Bowker—both the name and the company idea. In 1970, Bowker was a writer in Seattle making once-a-month jaunts to a coffee roaster called Murchie's in Vancouver, British Columbia. A true coffee connoisseur, Bowker found himself bringing back increasingly large loads of coffee with each 140-mile trek north. The coffee beans were purchased first for himself, then for friends, and, finally, for friends of friends. On one trip, the U.S. Customs agent gently explained to him the difference between shopping and smuggling. His solution was to start a coffee company.

Bowker shared his idea and brainstormed with friends Jerry Baldwin and Zev Siegl. The three shared similar interests—movies, literature, classical music, good food, wine, and the best coffee—and they were excited by the thought of bringing the best coffees to Seattle and opening a store in their own city. Their philosophy focused on educating their customers about quality coffee; then, the customers could take their coffee purchases home, grind the beans, and brew the grounds for themselves. Starbucks was born in that conversation on the lawn outside Siegl's Magnolia Bluff house.

Bowker's father had died when he was only three months old, leaving his mother to raise him alone. He graduated from O'Dea High School in Seattle and attended the University of San Francisco. Just eight course-hours short of his degree, he quit and did not graduate from college. Instead, Bowker traveled cross-country with friends, including Siegl. He followed that with a tour through Europe, where he acquired a fondness for beer and Italian espresso.

His odd jobs over the next few years included driving taxis, house-sitting, and guiding tours for Seattle Underground. Working as a writer in the late 1960s, a job for which he needed his caffeine fixes, he scripted educational films for a division of King Broadcasting and did freelance work for the original *Seattle* magazine. He also started an advertising company, Heckler Bowker.

Bowker's role during the start-up phase of Starbucks was in the marketing. He continued his day job but worked at the store on weekends. He even painted the first Starbucks store.

By the early 1980s, Bowker remained involved as a Starbucks owner, but he devoted more time to his other business ventures. He helped launch *Seattle Weekly* and cofounded the Redhook Ale Brewery.

Today, Bowker is an extremely successful entrepreneur who likes the challenge of launching start-ups. His Redhook brewery is a publicly traded company with sales of $41.5 million, and it is a well-known craft brewer in the United States. Redhook brews its beers in its two company-operated breweries—one in a suburb of Seattle and the other in Portsmouth, New Hampshire. It produces beer under a small number of brands, including its flagship Redhook ESB, styled after the Extra Special Bitters found in English pubs. Redhook's beers are distributed nationally, primarily by a distribution alliance with Anheuser-Busch, which owns about a third of the company. Redhook is in the process of merging its operations with Widmer Brothers Brewing of Portland.

After Bowker and Baldwin sold their Starbucks assets to Howard Schultz and his investor group in 1987, Bowker left the coffee business. He re-emerged in the caffeinated arena in 1994 and served on the board of Peet's Coffee & Tea from 1994 until May 2008. Peet's today is a publicly traded company based in Emeryville, California. The company has sales of about $250 million a year and 166 stores nationwide—most located on the West Coast. Peet's roasts and ships beans the same day, touting "Roaster-to-Cup" freshness.

Bowker lives in Seattle, and his best friend remains Starbucks cofounder Baldwin.

Coffee Talk

The world's five largest producers of coffee are Brazil, Colombia, Indonesia, Vietnam, and Mexico. The United States is the world's largest importer of coffee.

JERRY BALDWIN

Gerald "Jerry" Baldwin is a coffee man through and through. He was born in San Francisco and attended the University of San Francisco, where he roomed with Bowker and became friends with Siegl. Following college, Baldwin was an English teacher in the U.S. Army at Fort Ord in California. After his army stint, he and Siegl developed many business ideas, including shooting a series of film documentaries about ethnic music and starting a radio station featuring classical music, but none of their ideas came to fruition. It was not until Bowker brought up his frustration with the difficulties of finding good coffee that everything clicked. Baldwin's business life from that day on centered on coffee.

Alfred Peet introduced Baldwin to the fine art of coffee selecting, blending, and roasting in the early 1970s. He became an expert roaster, first with Starbucks and then with Peet's. He is currently a trustee for the Specialty Coffee Institute, an honorary member of the Kilimanjaro Specialty Coffee Growers Association, and a director and past president of the Association Scientifique Internationale du Café. In addition, Baldwin was a founding director of Redhook Ale Brewery. He was honored with the Lifetime Achievement Award by the Specialty Coffee Association of America, of which he is a past director. He is also a director of TechnoServe, a nonprofit association working to eliminate poverty in Latin America and Africa.

Baldwin was the company's first roaster and served as president of Starbucks until 1987, when the assets were sold to Schultz and investors. Baldwin and his cofounders also developed other Starbucks spin-off companies. Blue Anchor, for grocery market distribution, was sold to Milestone in 1981. Caravali Coffee, Starbucks' wholesale division, was sold in 1987, at the same time as the Starbucks sale. Even then, though, Baldwin wanted to remain in the coffee business and decided to retain Peet's Coffee & Tea.

He had fallen in love with the Peet's stores years before. Peet's, according to Baldwin, was the ultimate coffee experience. When he learned of the opportunity to buy Peet's in 1984, he was ecstatic; it was a long-held dream. The story goes that he quickly called Bowker to let him know that they were buying Peet's—no discussion. Bowker agreed that Peet's had the best coffee and provided a special place for customers to gather, so there was no argument from him.

Some of Baldwin's disenchantment with Starbucks no doubt came from disagreements with Schultz. Even before he hired him, Baldwin had misgivings, and it took more than a year for Schultz to land the job. Baldwin wanted to keep things small, and the ambitious Schultz knew the company was destined for a national presence, and then a global one. Baldwin did not go for the espresso bar concept, and there was constant stress at the Starbucks offices. He was also tired of going back and forth between Peet's and Starbucks, essentially running two companies.

In June 1987, the sale of Starbucks was complete, and any friendship between Baldwin and Schultz was beyond repair. Baldwin departed for Berkeley to maintain Peet's, leaving the coffeehouse he had helped create to its new CEO.

Since taking over his new business, Baldwin has focused on maintaining the legacy of Peet's as the master coffee roaster and authority it has always been. He works to consider employee involvement and creative thinking and encourages open communication with customers and employees. Baldwin and Peet's pride themselves on their loyal base of customers, dubbed *Peetnicks* for their devotion to high-quality, signature blend coffees.

Baldwin was president and CEO of Peet's from 1984 to 1994, and from 1994 to 2001 he served as chairman. When Peet's became a publicly traded company in 2001, he took the title of director. Under Baldwin's leadership, Peet's has flourished on its successful business journey by continuing to hand-roast its beans and providing suppliers with the highest-quality product.

ZEV SIEGL

The family of Zev Siegl was entrenched in the Seattle community. Both his parents were well-known Seattleites. Henry Siegl, his father, was a prominent violinist and concertmaster of the Seattle Symphony Orchestra. His mother, Eleanor Siegl, was a respected educator and founder of Bellevue's Little School. Both passed away in the late 1990s.

Siegl, Bowker, and Baldwin were acquainted from their college days at the University of San Francisco. In the early 1960s, Bowker and Siegl, along with another friend, even traveled cross-country together. Eventually, Siegl, Bowker, and Baldwin all settled in Seattle. After embracing the idea to create a coffee store named Starbucks, the trio decided Siegl would travel to the San Francisco area to investigate potential coffee roasters. Siegl visited several but decided that Peet's Coffee & Tea, which had become a favorite among loyal coffee drinkers since its opening in 1966, would be the best choice. All agreed, and Siegl soon began working in the Berkeley store to learn from Peet, the owner and master coffee roaster. Siegl wanted to learn all he could about coffee making, so he placed himself right in the store. Peet's approach to dark-roasting high-quality arabica coffee beans was an inspiration for the founders of Starbucks.

From 1971 to 1980, Siegl worked at Starbucks. Originally a tea drinker in the early 1970s (though he has since converted to espresso), he jumped on the idea of opening a coffee store. He had been looking for an excuse to quit his history teaching position and became Starbucks' first paid employee. Siegl, a people-person who enjoyed his customers, scooped coffee beans while extolling the virtues of quality coffee. He was the retail man and thrived in his position. But, in 1980, citing burnout and wanting to move on to other ventures, Siegl sold his portion of the business to Bowker and Baldwin.

For the past three decades, Siegl has busied himself with a wide spectrum of small-business activities. He cofounded both Quartermaine Coffee Roasters and Peerless Pie. Today, he is a full-time business development specialist for the publicly funded Small Business Development Center near Seattle. His mission is to help small- and medium-sized companies grow. Siegl provides confidential counseling to assist small-business owners, including assistance with starting a business, expanding, business planning, and selling or buying a company. He is an entrepreneur extraordinaire.

Siegl, Bowker, and Baldwin were a powerful trio who took the simple idea of bringing good coffee to Seattle and created a highly respected local roaster and coffee retailer. The stage was set for Schultz to enter the scene and move Starbucks onto a global voyage.

Coffee Talk

WHICH IS THE ONLY U.S. STATE THAT GROWS COFFEE?

Hawaii is the only state within the United States that produces coffee. Each of the five major islands produces 100 percent Hawaiian-grown arabica coffees. There are 6,500 acres of coffee trees in Hawaii, with an annual production of 6 million to 7 million pounds of green coffee beans.

Source: Hawaii Coffee Association.

HOWARD SCHULTZ

Ten years after Starbucks opened, Howard Schultz, a former vice president of U.S. operations for Hammarplast, a Swedish housewares firm, joined the company as director of marketing and operations. Schultz considered the Starbucks coffee bean stores groundbreaking and set out to convince Baldwin to hire him. He later noted, "At that time, I knew of no other high-end coffee bean stores in New York or any other city" (Schultz and Yang 1997, 39). Schultz's mother urged him not to give up a lucrative, high-powered New York position for a small firm that no one had ever heard of. Despite her concern, in the summer of 1982, Schultz and his wife, Sheri, packed up their car and drove 3,000 miles across the country to join the small coffee company with just five stores. With Schultz's visionary concepts, the wheels were set in motion to lead this local roaster and coffee retailer to become a global coffee empire.

Schultz, who recently earned upward of $10 million a year in compensation, had meager beginnings. He was born in Brooklyn, New York, in 1953, and he was raised in subsidized public housing in the Canarsie section of the borough. Schultz's father held a series of blue-collar jobs, from truck driver and cab driver to factory worker. Sometimes, he would work two or three jobs just to keep his family afloat. Watching his father's struggles, Schultz was determined to succeed. He attended Canarsie High School, where he excelled in sports and was the quarterback of the football team. Schultz then headed to Northern Michigan University on a football scholarship. He ended up not playing football at all, instead taking on part-time jobs and summer work to pay his college expenses. In 1975, Schultz became the first college graduate in his family.

His first job out of college was as a sales trainee for Xerox. He then went to Hammarplast to work in sales and eventually was promoted to vice president of U.S. operations. Shortly after joining Starbucks in 1983, Schultz made a trip to Milan and experienced the coffeehouses of Italy. They served espresso drinks and provided a social gathering place for customers. He brought the concept back to the three Starbucks owners, and they agreed to an experimental espresso bar in one downtown Seattle store. Despite its success, the original founders disagreed with Schultz about what Starbucks' focus and mission should be. They wanted to stick with selling their popular coffee beans, while Schultz tried to convince Bowker and Baldwin that more money could be made in operating coffeehouses than in targeting the home coffee market.

Schultz left Starbucks to open his own Il Giornale coffeehouse in 1986. In less than a year, Il Giornale had opened three locations, and in 1987, Schultz was given the opportunity to buy out his former employers—including the Starbucks Coffee name. He added the six Starbucks stores to his three Il Giornale stores and kept on growing.

Schultz's career in the new Starbucks started out with his role as chairman and CEO from 1987 to 2000; then, he changed to chairman and chief global strategist from 2000 to 2008. The move from executive to strategist was initiated by Schultz, who felt it was time to shift his position and allow the wisdom of others to prevail. Orin Smith followed as CEO until his retirement in 2005. Smith had joined Starbucks as vice president and chief financial officer in 1990, later serving as president and chief operating officer beginning in 1994.

The company went public in 1992. With Schultz at the reins, the company's growth multiplied faster than anyone could have dreamed. At the end of fiscal 1987, there were 17 stores; in 1992, 165; and by 2000, 3,501 stores. At the end of 2005, the number of stores had topped 10,000, and at the end of fiscal 2008 the company had 16,680 stores worldwide in 47 countries.

Schultz coauthored a book in 1997, titled *Pour Your Heart into It: How Starbucks Built a Company One Cup at a Time*. Schultz is also a former owner of the NBA's Seattle Supersonics. In 2006, he sold the team to a group of businessmen from Okalahoma City for $325 million. The Sonics, which had called Seattle home for 40-plus years, were moved to Oklahoma City starting with the 2008–09 season. The move was the result of a heated battle that left Schultz a less-than-favored son with sports enthusiasts in Seattle. He also owned the WNBA's Seattle Storm and cofounded Maveron, a Seattle venture fund.

On January 8, 2008, Schultz regained his status as CEO of Starbucks after eight years' hiatus, in order to address declining store traffic and depressed sales. He replaced Jim Donald, who had served as CEO since March 2005. Donald, who had previously served as president of the company's North American division, was replaced as part of a mass restructuring effort to help the struggling company rebound.

Schultz is married to Sheri Kersch Schultz, an interior designer. They live in Seattle with their two children.

Timeline: Howard Schultz, CEO of Starbucks

1953 Born July 19 in Brooklyn, New York.

1975 Graduated from Northern Michigan University with a bachelor of science degree.

1976 Joined Xerox as a salesman.

1978 Met interior designer and future wife Sheri Kersch over the July Fourth weekend in the Hamptons.

1979 Took a job in sales for Hammarplast; was eventually promoted to vice president and general manager in charge of U.S. operations.

1982 Employed by Starbucks as director of retail operations and marketing.

1985 Founded Il Giornale after leaving Starbucks. Its first Italian-style coffee bar opened the following year.

1987 Purchased Starbucks with a team of investors and returned to Starbucks as president and CEO.

1992 Led Starbucks to become the first publicly traded specialty coffee company.

1997 Penned *Pour Your Heart into It: How Starbucks Built a Company One Cup at a Time* with Dori Jones Yang. The book is a detailed business success story of how Starbucks grew from a single coffee store in Seattle to a worldwide cultural phenomenon.

2000 Became chairman and chief global strategist of Starbucks.

2001 Purchased the NBA's Seattle Supersonics; later sold the team to a group from Oklahoma City in 2006.

2008 Announced his return as Starbucks CEO on January 7, effective the next day.
Taking action to position the company with a solid foundation for long-term financial health, announced on July 1 that Starbucks would close approximately 600 company-operated stores in the United States.

DAVE OLSEN

Another early key player in the development of Starbucks is Dave Olsen. Olsen, who graduated from Montana State University with a bachelor of science degree, has been vital to the stellar growth of the Starbucks Corporation. He has long been a coffee lover. In the 1970s, he visited coffee bars in the San Francisco Bay Area, including Peet's Coffee & Tea in Berkeley. Olsen bought an espresso machine at Peet's and soon became an espresso fanatic and Peet's devotee.

In 1975, he moved to Seattle with the idea of opening his own espresso bar. He soon opened Café Allegro, which was a small coffee bar in the University District, located in the garage of a former mortuary. It was near the University of Washington campus and became a hangout for university professors and students. Olsen learned the retail business, spending time behind the counter serving customers, as well as hiring and training baristas. He searched for the best coffee beans and found them across town at Starbucks. The roasters at Starbucks helped him develop a custom espresso roast for Café Allegro, which is still sold in Starbucks stores today.

Upon hearing in the mid-1980s that Schultz was leaving Starbucks to establish a new coffeehouse, Olsen called Schultz and said he would like to work for the new company. He was interested in pursuing the Italian coffer bar concept and agreed to work cheap, starting with a salary of only $12,000 a year. He joined Il Giornale in 1986 and stayed through the transition to Starbucks Corporation. Soon, Olsen was responsible for traveling to find the best coffee beans in the world. Schultz noted, "Starbucks would not be what it is today if Dave Olsen hadn't been part of my team back at Il Giornale. He shaped its values, bringing a strong, romantic love for coffee, unshakable integrity, disarming honesty, and an insistence on authenticity in every aspect of the business" (Schultz and Yang 1997, 85).

Olsen is committed to giving back to the global community and has helped create programs aimed at improving quality of life for workers in coffee-growing areas of the world. He is a partner in the Seattle Initiative for Global Development, a group of business leaders who have banded together to provide active solutions to global poverty. Today, Olsen is senior vice president of culture and leadership development at Starbucks Coffee Company.

Coffee Pioneer Alfred Peet (1920–2007)

Alfred Peet, founder of Peet's Coffee & Tea, was an inspiration for Starbucks. He passed away on August 29, 2007, at his home in Ashland, Oregon. He was 87 years old and had lived a life devoted to specialty coffees and the unique dark-roasting style he helped make popular. Peet was born in Alkmaar, Holland, on March 10, 1920, the son of a Dutch roaster, and grew up helping his father in the business. After World War II, Peet apprenticed himself to Lipton's Tea in London as a tea taster and then ventured to Indonesia to work in the tea business. In 1955, he moved to San Francisco, where he took a job in the coffee importing industry.

Peet was troubled by the poor quality of coffee being brought into the United States, and thus the poor coffee being drunk by Americans. So Peet decided to open his own shop at Walnut and Vine streets in Berkeley, California, in 1966. With the opening of that one tiny store, the world of specialty coffee would never be the same. The gourmet coffee trend started on the West Coast and moved east to engulf the nation. Peet used superior-quality coffee beans and hand-roasted them, which gave the coffee its top-quality flavor. A gathering place for coffee connoisseurs, his business was frequented by University of California–Berkeley, faculty, students, intellectuals, and writers. The store flourished, and Peet soon opened additional shops in the San Francisco Bay Area. Peet's Coffee & Tea is still in operation today, and the original location is referred to as the Gourmet Ghetto. As of December 30, 2007, the company operated 166 retail stores in six states.

Peet taught others his unique style of roasting beans, which was quite different from that of the mainstream coffee companies. He used superior-quality beans, hand-roasted them in small batches, and developed a dark roasting style for richer flavor. Young Seattle entrepreneurs Jerry Baldwin, Gordon Bowker, and Zev Siegl asked Peet to provide his roasted coffee beans for their new coffee venture, Starbucks Coffee, Tea, and Spices, in 1971. He also served as a mentor, teaching the new businessmen his roasting technique.

Peet retired in 1983, and just one year later, the remaining two Starbucks partners (Siegl sold out in 1980), with a group of investors, bought Peet's four Bay Area locations. When Baldwin and Bowker sold Starbucks to Howard Schultz and his investors in 1987, Baldwin kept the original Peet's coffee shop, and the business continued to grow. In 2001, Peet's became a public company, trading on the NASDAQ.

YOU DECIDE

Is any one person worth multimillion-dollar compensation to a company? Schultz, founder of the new Starbucks Corporation and current president and CEO, is highly valued by his board. He was ranked fifth on *Forbes'* Top Paid CEOs of 2007 list, with a total compensation of almost $99 million. Now, most of his pay was earned from exercised stock options; nonetheless, his salary for that year was still $1.19 million.

If you were a board member and in a position to set the CEO's salary, what would you decide? Do you think it is prudent to approve such a high compensation package for Schultz? Is anyone worth $99 million a year to a company? One school of thought says high salaries are needed to retain top-quality executives to run profitable megacorporations. The other side thinks such salaries are excessive and greedy, and the funds could be better utilized to provide returns to shareholders, higher salaries for all employees, or lower prices for consumers. Here is an area where the experts disagree, and there are probably no right or wrong answers. Which side are you on?

Chapter Three

Strategies and Innovations: The Coffee Culture

Starbucks executives continue to respectfully and willingly share profits with their people. Through this sharing, partners appreciate the direct link between their effort and the success of the business enterprise.
—Joseph A. Michelli, *The Starbucks Experience: 5 Principles for Turning Ordinary into Extraordinary* (2007)

THE SHIFT TO COFFEE BARS

When Howard Schultz first decided to leave Starbucks in 1986, he was determined to shift from retail sales to see his coffee bar vision fulfilled. At the time, Schultz's parting from Starbucks was amiable; the departure was simply the result of a differing vision. Schultz had a goal of recreating the Italian coffeehouse culture, while Gordon Bowker and Jerry Baldwin were satisfied with the status quo and were not impressed with the experiment that placed espresso machines in their stores. They were dedicated to the old-fashioned retail side of selling coffee by the bag.

So Schultz moved on, starting Il Giornale. The first Il Giornale coffee bar was in the Columbia Seafirst Center, the tallest building in Seattle. Il Giornale thrived, while Starbucks remained at a standstill. Schultz opened another coffee bar shortly thereafter in Seattle, and a third one in Vancouver. The relationship between the companies was so cordial that Il Giornale sold Starbucks coffee in its stores. Schultz placed Dave Olsen in charge of his store operations.

Meanwhile, at Starbucks, morale was down and people were not happy. There was dissension among the staff. Employees felt management was not behind them anymore. Bowker and Baldwin had grown tired of the hassles created by business growth. The company had moved far beyond the founders' original goal of bringing quality arabica coffee beans to others. Bowker had developed interests in other ventures, and Baldwin's true love was the Peet's Coffee & Tea store. So they decided to keep Peet's and put Starbucks up for sale—the Seattle stores, the roasting plant, and the Starbucks name.

When Schultz heard the news, he could not pass up the opportunity to buy the company he felt had so much potential. Schultz got on board with his investors in Il Giornale to the tune of nearly $4 million for the six-unit Starbucks chain. Although the friendship between Schultz and his former employers would soon terminate, they sold to him. In 1987, the Il Giornale shops changed their names to Starbucks and the unified company became Starbucks Corporation. A new Starbucks was born.

After a 20-month sabbatical developing his own company, 34-year-old Schultz was back with Starbucks, now as president and CEO. Baldwin remained president of the now-separately owned and operated Peet's Coffee & Tea.

That same year, Starbucks began its national expansion boom by opening stores outside Seattle, in Vancouver and in Chicago. Chicago had a particularly tough opening day—the first store opened on the day of the stock market crash—but Chicagoans eventually took to the dark-roasted coffee. Of course, this was after Schultz learned the hard way that the store should not open up directly onto the street. The winter weather is too frigid in Chicago to do so. Chicagoans showed by their patronage that they'd much prefer a store that opened up into a lobby.

Starbucks' rocky beginnings as it expanded its market to new cities eventually turned into phenomenal growth. At the end of fiscal 1987, the Starbucks Corporation had 17 stores. Visionary Schultz promised investors in 1987 that Starbucks would open 125 stores in five years. Surpassing the goal, at the end of 1992, the company had opened 165 stores.

Coffee Talk

In 1987, one of the original Il Giornale investors proposed terms to buy Starbucks himself, and he wanted Howard Schultz to succumb to his terms. Fearing that all of his investors might go along with the other proposal, Schultz called in someone with clout to go along with him to the meeting about the proposal.

Guess who attended the meeting with Schultz? Bill Gates, Sr., father of Microsoft's founder, Bill Gates. The senior Gates was a lawyer, a prestigious Seattleite, and a towering six feet, seven inches tall.

In 1987, original founders Jerry Baldwin and Gordon Bowker sold Starbucks' six retail establishments, roasting plant, and name. Schultz put together an investment group, and every original investor in Il Giornale had an opportunity to invest in the purchase of Starbucks. The Il Giornale investors backed Schultz, along with almost all other investors that were approached. The purchase price for Starbucks was $3.8 million. The three-unit Il Giornale acquired the assets of Starbucks and changed its name to Starbucks Corporation.

At the helm, Schultz was free to incorporate his coffee bar dream into Starbucks. He wanted to recreate a true Italian-style coffee bar. In Italy, the coffee bar is a third place between work and home, where people can enjoy coffee and socialize, and this is what Schultz envisioned and made happen for Starbucks. His first coffee bar had a stately espresso machine as its centerpiece, and the bar concept was an instant hit. All service was initially stand-up, with no seating areas. It was quickly discovered, though, that Americans wanted chairs. Nonetheless, the coffee bar environment, with baristas educating consumers on Italian-style espresso, enabled Starbucks' growth to skyrocket.

QUALITY SPECIALTY COFFEE

Top-quality fresh-roasted, whole-bean coffee was, and is, the company's foundation. Peet's use of high-grade arabica beans, dark-roasted by a trained roaster, became the focus for Starbucks. Baldwin was the first roaster. The company uses costly methods but produces a trademark beverage. Since 1971, Starbucks has been driven to ethically source and roast the uppermost-quality arabica beans in the world. The company is both the world's leading roaster and leading retailer of specialty coffee. Roasting and sourcing its own beans allows the company to closely control the quality of its product. Currently, Starbucks has four established roasting plants: in Washington State, Pennsylvania, Nevada, and the Netherlands. In 2007, Starbucks broke ground in Sandy Run, South Carolina, on a 120,000-square-foot roasting facility, which opened in early 2009.

Starbucks' coffee buyers make it their mission to select only the highest-quality arabica beans. Buyers travel the world to Latin America, Africa, Arabia, and the Asia-Pacific region to select beans. Then, roasters take the beans and develop the rich, dark roast that is Starbucks' trademark.

First, green coffee beans are fired in a large, rotating drum. The first audible pop will occur after roughly 8 minutes in the roaster. The beans increase in size, roughly doubling. The coffee beans are now light brown in color. After 10 to 11 minutes in the roaster, the coffee beans become an even brown color. Usually, somewhere between 11 and 15 minutes in, the full flavor potential begins to build up in the beans. The listener will hear a second crack, which is really a group of forceful crackling noises. The dark roast begins and the great Starbucks flavor develops at the second crack.

Coffee Talk

Coffee trees grow roughly 40 feet high. Coffee plants produce cherry-like fruits, which contain two seed halves, called coffee beans. It is in the pit of the cherry that you will find the green, unroasted coffee bean.

ENTERTAINMENT

What could make your coffee experience even better? Starbucks believes listening to great music or reading an engrossing book while sipping its coffee heightens your enjoyment. Starbucks is so big on entertainment that it even has its own division—Starbucks Entertainment. The company began selling compact discs in 1995, as a result of a trendy in-house music program.

The idea to compile music to sell actually came from a partner, or Starbucks employee, Tim Jones. He was the store manager at University Village, one of the original Seattle locations. Jones had spent 20 years in the music business, proving Schultz's theory that partners have great insight and ideas.

Starbucks entered the music industry in 1999 with the acquisition of Hear Music, which began as a catalog company in 1990. Today, it is the Sound of Starbucks. Its hand-selected CDs and compilations are featured at Starbucks Cafes around the globe, online at www.hearmusic.com, and at the four Starbucks Hear Music Coffeehouses. The Hear Music stores are located in Miami, Florida; San Antonio, Texas; Santa Monica, California; and Bellevue, Washington. There, you will find the traditional coffeehouse experience, coupled with access to over one million digital songs and over 5,000 CDs in the physical music inventory. The company formed the Hear music label in 2007. The first artist signed to the record label was former Beatle Paul McCartney.

Starbucks also partnered in 2004 with Concord Records, which later produced a CD by Ray Charles called *Genius Loves Company*. One week after being released in the fall of 2004, the CD had sold 44,000 copies, and had risen to number two on the Billboard Charts.

In 2006, Starbucks teamed up with Apple, Inc., to set up a Starbucks section on Apple's iTunes store, offering music and video downloads. The following year, wireless communication became available between Apple and select Starbucks stores through AT&T Wi-Fi technology. This meant that customers with a computer could download music while listening to it in those stores. These days, screens at Starbucks display the song title, artist, and album name of music playing in the stores. If you hear a song you like, check out the "Now Playing" screen for artist details. Then, you can wirelessly buy and download music to your Apple iPhone, iTouch, or laptop computer.

Music isn't the only entertainment coffee lovers enjoy. Starbucks has branched out to experiment with a variety of entertainment media. It tried stepping into the movie arena, partnering with a film company to promote and sell DVDs in Starbucks stores. It has also started a very successful book program and offers select titles in its Starbucks Book Club. Three of the chain's selected books have hit number one on the *New York Times* Best Sellers List.

Coffee Talk

With over $10 billion in revenues, Starbucks is more than 40 times larger than the nation's second-largest specialty coffee company, Caribou Coffee. The publicly-traded company began in 1992 and has $254 million in annual revenues. There are 511 Caribou Coffee stores scattered over 19 states, Washington, D.C., and two international locations.

STORE OWNERSHIP

Starbucks stores are located in urban, suburban, and even some rural areas. Convenience is an important part of the strategy, so Starbucks obliges customers with a fast-paced lifestyle by providing plentiful drive-through opportunities and off-highway stores.

For much of the history of Starbucks, *franchising* was almost a dirty word in company ranks. Franchising is a form of business in which the owner of a product or service authorizes someone else to sell or distribute that company's goods or services, in return for monetary compensation. Although franchising is a common strategy for many firms that want quick, national expansion, Schultz was opposed to the business strategy for many years. He wrote, "If we had franchised, Starbucks would have

A typical sales area, this one in Peterborough, UK, showing a display of food and the beverage preparation area.

lost the common culture that made us strong" (Schultz and Yang 1997, 173). But, in 1991, the opportunity became too tempting, and an exception was made. Schultz concedes, "The opportunities to attract new customers were too appealing to pass up, and the window would not be open indefinitely. Each new venture, though, is part of an ongoing struggle."

The first big concession was in the airport arena. Seattle opened its first licensed airport store with HMHS Host, starting in Seattle and expanding to airports across the United States. During a period of transition and training, Starbucks worked diligently with HMHS Host employees until they grew more comfortable in Starbucks stores and became familiar with the products. Today, newly hired employees receive the same full 24 hours of training in the fine points of coffee beans, brewing, and customer service as all Starbucks employees.

In addition to its company-operated stores, Starbucks works with carefully selected businesses to operate licensed stores in a number of different types of establishments. Today, you might find Starbucks in select grocery stores, hotels, food-service companies, hospitals, churches, libraries, and military bases. The leadership team is very careful about the companies it chooses. Look for Starbucks in such places as Hyatt Hotels, U.S. Barnes & Noble Booksellers stores, United Airlines, Horizon Air, and Chicago's Wrigley Field.

Schultz Time!

Howard Schultz, Starbucks president and CEO, and chairman of the Starbucks Board of Directors, has been pivotal to the company's continuing success. See if you can fill in the blanks that led to the Coffee King's acquisition of Starbucks.

Schultz grew up in (1) _____. He attended (2) _____ _____ University on a football scholarship. In 1982, he joined Starbucks Coffee Company as the director of (3) _____. After a business trip to Milan, he was convinced that the (4) _____ bar concept would work for Starbucks, a thought not wholly supported by the original founding group. So he started his own coffee shop named (5) _____ in 1985, and two years later, the original founders sold the assets of Starbucks to Schultz and his investment group for a whopping (6) _____. The company has popularized high-quality (7) _____ coffee, tea, and specialty drinks. With Schultz's business skill and insight into consumers' desire for a social hub, the coffeehouse concept has driven Starbucks to become the world's (8) _____ retail gourmet coffee shop.

Answers: 1. New York; 2. Northern Michigan; 3. marketing; 4. espresso; 5. Il Giornale; 6. $3.8 million; 7. arabica; 8. largest.

COFFEE, TEA, AND MORE

Starbucks is known for its world-class arabica coffee, but if java is not your thing, Starbucks will probably still appeal to you. Tea lovers enjoy the wide variety of Tazo teas. The selection is available in stores and online at StarbucksStore.com. And the company has fine accessories galore: espresso machines, coffeemakers, coffee presses, grinders, tea presses, tea kettles, and more. Just enjoy water? In its coffeehouses, Starbucks sells Ethos bottled water. Ethos Water not only quenches thirst, but also has a social mission of helping children around the world get clean water. Hungry? Starbucks sells salads, sandwiches, and pastries in select markets.

Why Does Coffee Sometimes Make You Jumpy?

Coffee contains caffeine, which is a stimulant. Because coffee can provide a boost of energy, some people enjoy a cup or two to start their day. Still others might sip coffee as a pick-me-up later in the afternoon. Employees working the third shift can usually find a pot of coffee brewing to help them stay alert. Truck drivers may drink coffee to keep them awake during long drives. Even students, studying late into the night, may down a cup of coffee or two to help in a late-night study session.

But too much caffeine can raise your blood pressure, increase your heart rate, cause irritability, and keep you from sleeping. If you enjoy the taste of coffee, but it simply makes you too jumpy, you do have an alternative. Decaffeinated coffee is a great option, because decaffeination involves removing caffeine from coffee. Decaf is produced with products that extract the caffeine from the coffee beans. So, if you find coffee to be too invigorating, try one of the many decaf whole-bean or ground-bean varieties available.

REAL ESTATE DEAL MAKER

Location, location, location! It is a phrase made famous by the real estate industry, and Starbucks puts the motto into practice. According to Schultz, Starbucks is a third place between work and home. Likely, you will find a store in between on *your* commute. Store placement is a big deal for the company. Starbucks has a stellar record of placing stores where people will flock to them. Consider these staggering statistics: In the United States, Starbucks has operations in all 50 states, as well as the District of Columbia. There are 7,238 company stores and 4,329 licensed stores.

GLOBAL EXPANSION

Starbucks began its overseas expansion in 1996, starting in Tokyo. Adding to its growing international influence, in 1998, the Starbucks Corporation acquired the Seattle Coffee Company of Britain. Its 60 stores were given the Starbucks name, and the company had an instant presence in that country. The company now has over 5,000 coffeehouses in 46 countries outside the United States. In 2003, roasting operations began outside of the United States, as well. A new roasting plant was built that year in Amsterdam, the Netherlands. The company's development strategy adapts to different international markets, staying aware of local needs. There are three business strategies used—joint ventures, licensed shops, and company-owned operations. Internationally, there are 1,979 company-operated stores and 3,134 licensed stores. Table 3.1 shows the countries around the world where Starbucks has a presence.

While its main goal is protecting the quality of Starbucks coffee, the company is adaptable to cultural issues and social norms. There are over 700 stores in Japan, but adaptations were made. Stores there provide

Table 3.1
Starbucks' Presence around the World (2009)

Argentina	Hawaii	Puerto Rico
Australia	Hong Kong S.A.R.	Qatar
Austria	Indonesia	Romania
The Bahamas	Ireland	Russia
Bahrain	Japan	Saudi Arabia
Brazil	Jordan	Singapore
Canada	Kuwait	South Korea
Channel Islands	Lebanon	Spain
Chile	Malaysia	Switzerland
Cyprus	Mexico	Taiwan
Czech Republic	The Netherlands	Thailand
Denmark	New Zealand	Turkey
Egypt	Oman	United Arab Emirates
France	People's Republic of China	United Kingdom
Germany	Peru	United States
Greece	The Philippines	

Source: Starbucks.com

green tea Frappuccinos, smaller cup sizes, and smaller pastries to suit the Japanese preferences. Asian markets have more savory foods to adapt to different tastes. Most of the changes are minor adaptations, but in Saudi Arabia, for example, all stores are segregated into men-only and family sections, respecting the country's rigid rules for separation of the sexes in public places.

Starbucks Brings More Coffee to Europe

The $10 billion coffee king, Starbucks, along with the $42 billion Kraft Foods, an industry leader in the food and beverage industry, have together expanded their offerings in Europe. This business unit began selling packaged coffee and single-insert Tassimo discs (T-discs) in select supermarkets in France and Germany in spring 2009. Starbucks had started selling its packaged coffee products in Europe in 2007, launching in the United Kingdom. The next year, it introduced the line in Switzerland and Ireland.

Europeans have long enjoyed their coffee, and the Starbucks and Kraft megacompanies hope to cash in on the coffee-drinking craze. "Europe has a strong, vibrant coffee culture, and we're proud to contribute to its richness by offering consumers super-premium Starbucks coffee for at-home brewing," said Rich DePencier, vice president of Starbucks Global Consumer Products International in a March 5, 2009, news release. "Our consumer products business is important to the overall success of the company, and we are committed to bringing the Starbucks Experience to consumers throughout Europe at our retail stores and in supermarkets."

Grocery store sales could be extremely profitable and a wise strategy. The press release notes that revenues from roast and ground coffee in western Europe in 2007, according to Datamonitor, totaled $8.9 billion, and sales are expected to rise to approximately $10 billion by the end of 2012. Starbucks currently has 48 coffeehouses in France and 140 coffeehouses in Germany.

Starbucks and Kraft Foods announced their agreement to sell Starbucks coffee in grocery stores in 1998. This is a duo that has proven profitable and successful. Starbucks has the premium coffee product, and Kraft has the skill in marketing and distribution to grocery retailers. Today, the firms provide customers with Starbucks whole-bean and ground coffees and Tassimo T-discs in the United States, Canada, the United Kingdom, Ireland, Switzerland, France, and Germany.

ICE CREAM, COFFEE BEVERAGES, AND TREATS

Starting in 1995, Starbucks expanded its horizons to include some new refreshments. Frappuccino blended drinks were the first specialty—blended beverages available in a variety of flavors. The next year, in 1996, the North American Coffee Partnership, a joint venture between Starbucks and Pepsi-Cola North America, began selling bottled Frappuccino drinks.

Starbucks Coffee teamed up with Dreyer's Grand Ice Cream during that same time to create a super-premium line of coffee ice creams. Then, Starbucks Corporation and Unilever, in fall 2008, entered an exclusive licensing agreement to market and distribute Starbucks ice cream in the United States and Canada, replacing the Dreyer's coffee flavors. The ice cream is made with real, brewed Starbucks coffee that is cooled down to creamy perfection. A new line of super-premium ice cream is available nationwide as of spring 2009. The four flavors are Caramel Macchiato, Mocha Frappuccino, Java Chip Frappuccino, and simple Coffee. The ice cream is not sold in Starbucks coffeehouses—most do not have freezers—and the company does not plan to sell the delicious treat in-house any time soon. The ice cream is exclusive to the grocery market.

Starbucks and Kraft entered into a licensing agreement in 1998 that was designed to accelerate the movement of Starbucks coffee into grocery stores. Today, you'll see the Starbucks name in most major grocery stores across the United States.

The company stays current in today's world by continuing to roll out amazing new treats, like hot and cold espressos, fabulous tea lattes, Frappuccino blended drinks, exceptional cocoas, Vivanno Nourishing Blends, chocolates, and energy drinks. There's sure to be more to come.

Try Out a Job: Market Research Analyst

One job you may want to consider is that of a market research analyst. Let's face it—it's never too early to start thinking about your career choices. Okay, so you would actually need a college degree, but let's pretend you have already snagged this job. A market research analyst would typically have a bachelor's degree in business with an emphasis in either marketing or economics. Higher education, such as a master's degree or a Ph.D. in marketing or statistics, would be helpful for moving up the corporate ladder. Strong statistical skills are essential for analyzing surveys and data. But enough about that. Let's say you have landed the job as assistant market research analyst at Shirley's Superior Surveys, Inc.

Market research analysts are interested in potential sales of a product or service. According to the Bureau of Labor Statistics' 2008–2009 Occupational Outlook Handbook, "Market, or marketing, research analysts help companies understand what types of products people want and at what price. They also help companies market their products to the people most likely to buy them. Gathering statistical data on competitors and examining prices, sales, and methods of marketing and distribution, they analyze data on past sales to predict future sales."

Analysts gather this data via a number of different methods, such as telephone surveys, mail surveys, or even personal interviews. Market research analysts in the coffee industry might survey a group of people to determine the number of coffee consumers versus the number of soda consumers. They could run a taste test on a new blend of coffee, or they might evaluate the impact of a pre-launch coffee flavoring on coffee purchasers. If you like people, products, and numbers, hop aboard, because you have found your niche.

For your first job assignment, Shirley, the CEO and head honcho, just wants to give you a feel for the business. So she assigns you a fun, informal job where you are able to talk to a lot of different people and ask them about their taste preferences. Shirley often does this with newbies, just to see how they respond, so be sure to take it seriously. Your assignment is to spend the next week—a full seven days—observing the number of people you see in your environment drinking retail coffee. (Hint: You can tell by the cup if it is from Starbucks, McDonald's, Dunkin' Donuts, etc.) The only exclusion is that if you visit an actual coffeehouse, it doesn't count. No cheating, please. As you maneuver through your daily routine—at school, at play, attending athletic events or church activities—chart the number of people drinking Starbucks coffee. Contrast this number with the total number of people you count drinking other specialty-brand coffees.

Another part of the assignment is to talk to some of the people you see drinking Starbucks coffee and ask them what they like about it. Exactly why do they buy Starbucks? Remember, you're an assistant market research analyst new to the job, so Shirley is going to be checking out your interpersonal skills.

1. How many Starbucks cups did you see?
2. How many other coffeehouse cups did you count?
3. How many other coffee cups did you count (from fast-food restaurants, etc.)?
4. List the various responses as to why people prefer Starbucks coffee.

I tried this informal survey myself, just for fun, and the number of Starbucks drinkers I observed was overwhelming. After a typical week of teaching college classes, shopping at the mall, attending athletic events with my children, and going to church activities, I was truly convinced of the popularity of the Starbucks brand. I tabulated 28 Starbucks drinkers and 2 others (which shall remain nameless). Comments as to why people drink Starbucks included, "I love it and don't drink anything else," and "Starbucks is my favorite coffee. I'm addicted." I have one student who has carried a Starbucks coffee cup every time I have seen him in class. He explained, "I have Starbucks several times a day and can find a coffee shop pretty much on any side of town." Consumers clearly love their Starbucks coffee, and those consumers are guaranteed consistency—the same taste and the same quality, whether they buy on a different side of town or in a different part of the country. That consistency, along with Starbucks' high quality, is part of the appeal of the brand name.

Chapter Four

Guiding Principles and Coffee Social Responsibility

Early on at Starbucks, we quickly figured out that when there was pain—economic pain, conflict, or disappointment over a failed idea—our hat was still our hat, our values were still our values, and sticking with them was the most important thing we could do.

—Howard Behar, former president, Starbucks International,
*It's Not about the Coffee: Leadership Principles from a
Life at Starbucks* (2007)

THE STARBUCKS EXPERIENCE

Going to Starbucks is definitely an experience, a third place between work and home where customers can find superior coffee and a place to relax or socialize with friends. The Starbucks experience is referenced in press releases and Starbucks literature. On the Starbucks Web site, the About Us section explains, "Through our unwavering commitment to excellence and our guiding principles, we bring the unique Starbucks experience to life for every customer through every cup." Memos from leader Howard Schultz and other partners constantly extol the virtues of the Starbucks experience. It permeates the culture of the company.

One thing is clear—it *is* all about the customer. Starbucks combines quality products with building a personal relationship with each customer. Schultz explains, "At Starbucks, our product is not just great coffee but also what we call the 'Starbucks experience': an inviting, enriching environment in our stores that is comfortable and accessible, yet also stylish and elegant" (Schultz and Yang 1997, 251). As of fiscal year-end 2008, roughly 176,000 employees were bringing the Starbucks experience to life in over 16,000 stores worldwide. The company strives to build a personal relationship with each of its customers.

COFFEE SOCIAL RESPONSIBILITY

Starbucks is a champion of stellar business practices that strive for social, environmental, and economic benefits for the communities where

The Starbucks Center, in Seattle, company headquarters, dates back to 1912, when Sears, Roebuck and Co. opened a catalogue distribution center. The building was hit by the Nisqually Earthquake in early 2001, causing extensive damage to the structure. Renovations and repairs were completed and the building was formally rededicated on September 20, 2002. At over 1.8 million square feet, Starbucks Center is the largest building in Seattle, and both the largest and oldest building in the country to earn a national green certification for existing buildings.

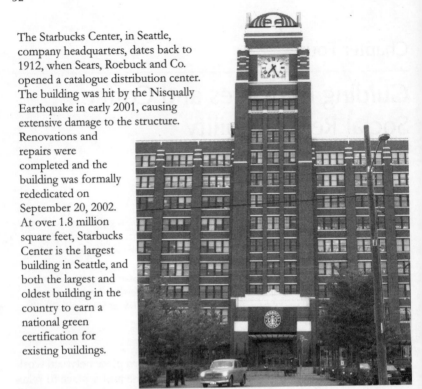

it does business. The Company Fact Sheet states, "Starbucks focuses its efforts on providing a great work environment for partners (employees); making a positive contribution to our communities; working with coffee farmers to help ensure their long-term success; and minimizing our environmental impact" (February 2008).

GREAT WORKPLACE ENVIRONMENT

It should be no surprise that many people want to work at Starbucks. Starbucks was ranked seventh among *Fortune Magazine*'s 100 Best Companies to Work For in 2008. Such a high ranking is rightfully earned. The employees Starbucks hires are called *partners,* and the company focuses on its partners, providing opportunities to develop skills, advance careers, and achieve goals. Starbucks has approximately 143,000 U.S. partners.

Part-time employees constitute two-thirds of the workforce for Starbucks. They are essential to the company's success and thus are treated with respect. Starbucks offers a multitude of benefits to its eligible full-time and part-time partners, including health care benefits, discounted stock purchase plans, and stock options, cleverly referred to as Bean Stock.

Starbucks' total pay package is referred to as Your Special Blend, because each partner has a unique situation and can make choices within his pay package based on needs and interest. An added plus—all partners get a pound of coffee a week.

Starbucks' Mission Statement reflects the company's strong desire to connect with people. The Our Partners section of the mission notes, "We're called partners, because it's not just a job, it's a passion." Imagine what a powerful impact such enthusiasm has on customer service. Each partner participates in training, which instills strong coffee education, product expertise, and excellent customer service.

The Starbucks Mission

To inspire and nurture the human spirit—one person, one cup, and one neighborhood at a time.

Source: Starbucks Company Web site, www.starbucks.com.

Baristas are the core of the coffee business. The baristas take the lead as they wait on people and work to provide an exceptional customer experience. They custom-mix drinks and explain the origins of different coffees. Starbucks' success is dependent on patrons having a very positive experience in its stores. Partners must not only have the skill and personality to communicate well with customers, but also be knowledgeable about the company's products.

Baristas go through 20 hours of training. The Starbucks management training program involves an additional 10 weeks. Training for in-store development managers is referred to as Boot Camp—a required one-week overview of developing a new Starbucks store. Boot Camp is conducted at headquarters in Seattle, and it is a total immersion in the company. Participants learn how the real estate team chooses sites, about construction budgets and the design and layout of a store, about IT support systems, how to purchase materials, equipment, and furniture, and more.

The pay and perks at the coffee company are good. The number-seven *Fortune* ranking among the best companies to work for shows the facts. The most common salaried job is the store manager, with an average annual paycheck of $45,713. The most common hourly-rate employee is a Coordinator II, at $37,390 average annual pay. Job sharing, a compressed work week, and telecommuting are a few more perks in the work life at Starbucks. As a result, people do want to work at Starbucks: 705,195 people applied in the 2008 ranking study. The voluntary turnover rate is just 13 percent for the year, relatively small in the business world and much lower than for similar retail coffee businesses.

A Starbucks barista.

CONTRIBUTING TO COMMUNITIES

Starbucks has developed a reputation over the years as a team player. The company is dedicated to making positive contributions to the communities where it does business—it's part of the Starbucks culture. You will regularly find Starbucks partners being good neighbors and giving back to their communities and neighborhoods. Starbucks offers a sizeable workforce to make the world a better place to live. In fact, in 2007, Starbucks partners and customers in the United States and Canada logged 320,000 volunteer hours. And there has been no slowdown since then, as Starbucks has set a powerful goal of contributing more than 1 million hours of community service each year, by the year 2015. Over the years, the company has addressed a multitude of causes, but it focuses on three main areas—literacy, environment, and poverty elimination. Partners are active and responsible neighbors in the areas where they live, work, and play. Starbucks believes that "doing good makes good business sense." (*Starbucks Corporation*). Starbucks stores open their doors for community and philanthropic events.

CEO Schultz donated the proceeds of his 1997 book, *Pour Your Heart into It*, in order to start the Starbucks Foundation. At the start, the foundation focused on funding literacy programs and nontraditional education programs. It has since grown by leaps and bounds. The Starbucks

Foundation is involved in championing education and youth leadership programs in towns where Starbucks operates, as well as making social investments in coffee-growing communities. The foundation has provided more than $22 million in grants to benefit people across the globe. Today, the foundation is largely funded by Starbucks and private donations.

CONTRIBUTING TO LEARNING

Starbucks became a partner and financial supporter of Jumpstart in 2001. The company's leaders wanted to be involved in the powerful impact Jumpstart has had in the field of early-childhood education. The nonprofit organization, headquartered in Boston, brings together at-risk preschoolers and adult volunteers who help them build the essential skills they need to enjoy future success in school.

Starbucks Partners with Jumpstart

James Cleveland, president of Jumpstart, discussed the importance of the organization and its partnership with Starbucks:

WHAT IS JUMPSTART?

Jumpstart is a national early education organization that works toward the day every child in America enters school prepared to succeed. By pairing nearly 4,000 trained adult mentors with underserved pre-schoolers for a full school year, Jumpstart helps children develop the language, literacy, and social skills they'll need to thrive in kindergarten and beyond. Working alongside parents and families, Jumpstart is currently serving nearly 15,000 children across 20 states, in partnership with more than 300 early learning centers and 74 universities and colleges throughout the country. Jumpstart's national sponsors include American Eagle Outfitters, AmeriCorps, Pearson, Sodexo, and Starbucks. Jumpstart is a five-time recipient of the *Fast Company/ Monitor Group Social Capitalist Award* (2004–2008) and has received a four-star rating from Charity Navigator. For more information, visit the Jumpstart Web site at www.jstart.org.

HOW DOES THE JUMPSTART MODEL WORK?

At Jumpstart, our goal is to build literacy, language, social, and initiative skills in young children. We do this by pairing motivated college students, called corps members, with preschool children in caring and supportive one-to-one relationships for an entire school year. Our model is designed to achieve three primary goals:

- **School success**—The one-to-one relationships at the core of the Jumpstart model build literacy in combination with social and emotional readiness. Time and again, we've seen how consistent, committed, and caring relationships prepare children for school and help to create a lifelong love of learning.

- **Family involvement**—Jumpstart focuses on three areas of family involvement: strong relationships, ongoing and consistent communication, and the Jumpstart-home learning connection. Jumpstart provides learning activities for the home, thereby reinforcing the learning that takes place during Jumpstart sessions.
- **Future teachers**—By working with college students, we are also helping to create new generations that are not only excited about early-childhood education, but also have developed the skills to make a difference. For eight months each year, our college student corps members attend twice-weekly, two-hour Jumpstart sessions at a preschool. Each of these sessions consists of three elements:
- *One-to-one reading:* Children choose books to read with their corps members, and the corps members use the dialogic reading method. In this method, a natural rhythm is established, promoting both reading and more in-depth discussion.
- *Circle time:* In a large-group setting, corps members lead children in activities that combine literacy, language, and social interaction, such as singing, finger-plays, and movement games. During circle time, children are welcomed and made to feel like a part of the Jumpstart community.
- *Choice time:* During this longest period of the Jumpstart session, each child creates a plan and chooses where to play. Corps members guide the children to develop and carry out their plans and to review at the end of each session. During choice time, children may also participate in small-group activities. These activities, which are planned by corps members, provide opportunities to experiment and solve problems in ways that are meaningful to each preschool child.

In addition to these Jumpstart sessions, corps members also spend two to five hours per week in classroom assistance time (CAT). During this time, corps members provide support not only to their partner children, but also to the classroom teachers. CAT allows Jumpstart to reach more children than those who participate in one-to-one sessions and also allows corps members to gain valuable early-childhood education experience.

WHEN DID STARBUCKS FIRST PARTNER WITH JUMPSTART?

The Starbucks Foundation signed on for a four-year, $1 million partnership with Jumpstart in April 2001. Building upon the success of this four-year partnership, it committed to renew its support in 2005, with cash and in-kind contributions totaling $1.5 million over three years.

HOW HAS STARBUCKS SUPPORTED JUMPSTART OVER THE YEARS?

In addition to the financial support mentioned above, Starbucks also sold Mitch Albom's book *For One More Day* in stores nationwide in 2007. Jumpstart received $1 from each sale, totaling nearly $100,000. In 2006, Starbucks provided major campaign support for Jumpstart's Read for the Record. Jumpstart's special edition of *The Little Engine That Could* was sold in more than 5,000 company-operated Starbucks stores during August 2006; 100 percent of the proceeds from sales were donated to Jumpstart.

The nonprofit also received incremental revenue from in-store marketing programs with Starbucks card reloads and activations of Starbucks Duetto Visa cards. Local seasonal Starbucks promotions, such as the St. Patrick's Day Leprechaun Latte for Literacy, also helped raise money and awareness for Jumpstart.

By placing advertisements in the *New York Times* and the *Boston Globe*, and by providing letters of support on behalf of Jumpstart, Starbucks helps Jumpstart influence national thought and discussions about early education.

In addition, in communities all across the United States, Starbucks partners with Jumpstart sites to host reading programs and book drives in Starbucks stores. It has also built children's libraries for neighborhoods served by Jumpstart.

IN 2009, HOW DOES THE COLLABORATION CONTINUE?

For the past seven years, Starbucks has been a strong advocate for Jumpstart's mission and a key supporter of the thousands of adults who have served as Jumpstart Corps members. During this period the Starbucks Foundation has provided more than $2.5 million in cash and in-kind donations to support Jumpstart's work. Additionally, Starbucks partners (employees) have collaborated with Jumpstart staff to create innovative national, regional, and local events to raise awareness and funding for Jumpstart, including playing a key role in the first Jumpstart Read for the Record campaign, and the ongoing popular Leprechaun Latte for Literacy Campaign. This year, Starbucks is providing significant financial support to Jumpstart programs in our Northeast, Mid-Atlantic, and Western regions, and we are extremely grateful for the ongoing partnership and belief in our work. Nationally, Starbucks continues to be engaged with Jumpstart as a valued thought partner.

The partnership between Starbucks and Jumpstart planted a seed that grew into a company-wide interest in education and a campaign to encourage public participation in literacy programs. Starbucks made its first voyage into helping international literacy in 2005, when the Starbucks Foundation pledged $5 million to support educational programs in China. The China Education Project demonstrates the coffee company's commitment to China, a market it entered in 1999. Since that time, partners in the China Starbucks stores have supported programs in their communities, including volunteer opportunities with local schools, as well as fundraising efforts to support AIDS-afflicted orphans, educational organizations, and tsunami victims.

Other ongoing Starbucks Foundation programs include projects that benefit coffee-, tea- and cocoa-growing communities; the Ethos Water Fund that supports access to clean water, sanitation, and hygiene education; Gulf Coast Recovery to assist in the recovery and rebuilding after hurricanes Rita and Katrina; and the Global Young Social Entrepreneurs program, which helps young social entrepreneurs advance in communities around the globe.

Starbucks' China Business Booms

You probably remember from your history text that in the late 1970s, China began a series of economic reforms, transitioning from a country with a centrally planned government to a market-oriented economy. The reforms have spurred international trade and a growing private sector. During this economic transformation, China packed on some powerful economic statistics.

Here is a quick look at the country. Gross Domestic Product (GDP) measures the output of a nation's economy—the total market value of all final goods and services produced within a country during a given time frame. China's economy has experienced stellar growth since the reforms began, and for 2008, it had a real GDP growth rate of a healthy 9 percent. To contrast this number, the Bureau of Economic Analysis posted a revised real GDP number of 1.1 percent for the U.S. economy.

According to the 2008 estimates from the *CIA World Factbook*, China is the third-largest economy in the world at $4.2 trillion (the United States is number one at $14.3 trillion, and Japan stands at $4.8 trillion; The World Factbook, 2009). Although China's real GDP is expected to dampen slightly due to the global recession, projections nevertheless forecast growth to remain strong and in positive territory. China is the world's most populous nation with 1.3 billion people, has a jobless rate of only 4 percent, and is one of the world's fastest-growing economies. Enter Starbucks.

Starbucks has been operating in China for 10 years, and business is booming. It opened its first stores in Taiwan in 1998 and in mainland China at the China World Trade Building in Beijing in 1999.

As of early 2009, there are over 690 stores in Greater China, which includes the People's Republic of China, Taiwan, Hong Kong, and Macau. Starbucks has more than 230 stores in 22 cities in mainland China alone. In fiscal 2008, Starbucks opened 37 new stores in China. Even as sales suffer in the United States and other areas of the globe due to the recessionary glut, Starbucks thrives in China.

In early 2009, Starbucks launched its first local coffee blend in China. The new coffee will be made in China's southwestern province of Yunnan, bordering Vietnam, Laos, and Myanmar. The new coffee is grown by farmers in China and comes from beans sourced from the Yunnan province. According to the Associated Press, the coffee, which the company hopes to bring to stores all over the world, is called South of the Clouds, which is the meaning of *Yunnan* in Chinese.

According to the Starbucks China Web site, www.starbucks.com.cn/, "Taking a long-term vision in China, Starbucks remains confident in its success in the Chinese market, as it views itself as a 'different kind of company' which is developing in China exactly at the time when the Chinese people are looking for more leisure lifestyle and when the company ideals mesh perfectly with China's aspiration to develop a 'harmonious society'" (About Starbucks, Starbucks in China). The new Chinese coffee and the Chinese economy both present exciting expansion opportunities for Starbucks.

SUPPORTING SUSTAINABLE COFFEE PRODUCTION

Coffee farming must be profitable to be sustainable. The concern, just as with any other agricultural product, is that if coffee farming is not a money-maker, the farmers may switch to growing other crops. Starbucks is doing its part to make sure coffee farming stays profitable.

Starbucks works together with farmers according to a plan that benefits both when it comes to coffee purchasing. The company's integrated approach to coffee purchasing is based on six fundamental principles, stated in the *Company Profile* (February 2008), that include "Paying premium prices for premium coffee to help farmers make profits and support their families," and "Encouraging participation in C.A.F.E. (Coffee and Farmer Equity) Practices, our social and environmental guidelines for coffee purchasing." Starbucks also buys conservation and certified coffee, makes funds available for credit to farmers, invests in social development projects in coffee-growing communities, and collaborates with other coffee leaders.

In fiscal 2007, world prices for arabica coffee beans averaged $1.14 per pound. Yet, Starbucks paid an average price of $1.43 per pound in a similar time frame. Why? The company is committed to paying the higher prices that high-quality arabica coffee demands. The higher prices paid by the Starbucks buyers provide coffee farmers some protection against drops in the coffee market. Case in point—in 2001, world arabica prices hit a record low of 42 cents per pound. The price hovered in that area for several years and created hardships for coffee farmers. Today's market conditions are greatly improved, and Starbucks' work at promoting sustainable production has assisted in this area.

Starbucks has its own self-imposed social and environmental guidelines for coffee purchasing, called the Coffee and Farmer Equity (C.A.F.E.) Practices Program. The company has made a huge impact on coffee growers with these practices. The program includes a set of independently verified guidelines to make certain that purchased coffee is grown and processed in an environmentally and socially responsible manner. When suppliers apply for C.A.F.E. Practices, they must go through an independent third-party evaluation. There are currently 28 organizations that act as verifiers for C.A.F.E. Practices.

Starbucks has been working to build a coffee sustainability model for 10 years, but it just formally introduced the C.A.F.E. Practices Program in fiscal 2004. Although detailed, the basic fundamentals of C.A.F.E. practices include product quality, economic accountability, social responsibility, and environmental leadership. The program includes a wide range of suppliers, from small family farms to large estates, as well as firms that mill and process coffee. Starbucks had a goal of purchasing 225 million pounds of green (unroasted) coffee in fiscal 2007 from C.A.F.E. Practices suppliers. The company exceeded the goal with 228 million pounds. This was approximately 65 percent of all coffee purchased by Starbucks that year. Starbucks is well on its way to a goal of 80 percent of its coffee coming from C.A.F.E. Practices suppliers by fiscal 2013.

Starbucks certainly acknowledges the importance of purchasing certain third party–certified coffees, particularly organic and Fair Trade Certified. Fair Trade products appeal to the socially minded consumer, because the certification assures the buyer that farmers receive an equitable price for their coffee and have access to international markets. Through this means, Starbucks is positively impacting the lives of many small farmers (see the box on Fair Trade Certified Coffee). The company has steadily increased its purchases of Fair Trade Certified coffee each year, and it will double its 2009 purchases to 40 million pounds. This makes the company the largest purchaser of Fair Trade Certified coffee in the world.

Certified Organic Coffee is a tough certification to receive. "Certified organic coffee is grown without the use of pesticides, herbicides, or chemical fertilizers, maintaining healthy soil and groundwater" (*Starbucks Corporation: Corporate Social Responsibility Fiscal 2007 Annual Report*, 13). Many coffees purchased by Starbucks are organically grown but do not bear the formal certification. The reason behind this is most likely the expense for small farmers to obtain the certification, as they must verify their use of

Coffee beans being sorted and pulped by workers and volunteers on an organic fair-trade, shade-grown coffee plantation in Guatemala.

organic farming methods. Yet a total of four percent of Starbucks coffee purchases is Certified Organic Coffee.

Often, small farmers experience a cash crunch and have to sell their crop to a local buyer for the best price they can get. Starbucks is a stellar corporate citizen. The company has worked with several financing organizations that make loans to coffee grower associations so they can sell their crops for a more favorable price. The company has committed $10.5 million to three not-for-profit organizations—the Calvert Foundation (see the box on Access to Credit), Verde Ventures Loan Fund, and Root Capital—in order to improve farmers' livelihood.

Starbucks believes in social development projects and knows that careful investment of its resources to help sustain coffee farms and fortify surrounding communities is beneficial. As an example, company investments in coffee community projects totaled $1.5 million in fiscal 2007. These funds helped pay for 50 projects located in 11 countries and aided more than 50,000 local farmers, their families, and their communities.

Starbucks collaborates with others in the coffee industry, strengthening the coffee supply chain. This network includes international groups, nongovernmental agencies, and public agencies that help address the turbulent challenges faced by coffee farmers and their communities. Starbucks participates in forums and commonly shares its C.A.F.E. Practices with others. Starbucks' collaborative nature has led to the United Nations Global Compact to Profile C.A.F.E. Practices. The company recognizes the importance of building up its overall business web, from the coffee farmers all the way to the consumers—the Starbucks customers.

Fair Trade Certified Coffee

The relationship between TransFair USA and Starbucks began in 2000, when Starbucks committed to sourcing, roasting, and selling Fair Trade Certified coffee. The two organizations share a common objective: to ensure that small-scale coffee farmers receive an equitable price for their commodity. But it is not just coffee that is Fair Trade Certified; many products are now being produced and sold under Fair Trade standards. The banana you had for breakfast or the chocolate bar you will snack on after school could be Fair Trade Certified.

Are you interested in socially responsible purchasing? Katie Barrow, public relations manager for TransFair USA, provided some details about the organization and the Fair Trade Certified label:

WHAT IS THE TRANSFAIR ORGANIZATION?

TransFair USA, a 501(c)(3) nonprofit organization, is one of more than 20 members of Fairtrade Labelling Organizations International (FLO) and the only third-party certifier of Fair Trade products in the United States. We audit transactions between U.S. companies offering Fair Trade Certified products and the international suppliers from whom they source, in order to guarantee that the farmers and farm workers behind Producers of Fair Trade Certified goods were paid a fair, above-market price. In addition, annual inspections conducted by FLO ensure that strict socio-economic development criteria are being met and that social premiums are paid to the farming cooperatives to fund community-elected development projects. TransFair USA certifies coffee, tea, cocoa, chocolate, sugar, vanilla, rice, bananas, flowers, honey, and wine.

FLO is the body that sets Fair Trade Certified standards and supports producers to gain and retain their Fair Trade Certified status. A separate organization, FLO-CERT, inspects and audits producers and traders against the standards.

WHAT IS FAIR TRADE CERTIFIED?

Fair Trade Certified is an innovative, market-based approach to sustainable development that helps small-scale farmers and workers in developing countries gain direct access to international markets.

Fair Trade Certified products directly support a better life for farming families in the developing world through fair prices, access to direct trade, community development, and environmental stewardship. Fair Trade farmers market their own harvests through direct, long-term contracts with international buyers, learning how to bootstrap their businesses and compete in the global marketplace. This empowerment lifts farming families from poverty through trade—not aid—keeping food on the table, children in school, and families on their land.

By the end of 2007, there were 632 Fair Trade Certified producer organizations in 58 producing countries, representing 1.5 million farmers and workers. With their families and dependents, FLO estimates that 7.5 million people directly benefit from Fair Trade.

Fair Trade Certified principles include the following:

Fair price: Democratically organized farmer groups receive a guaranteed minimum floor price and premiums specifically earmarked for community development projects; even higher premiums are given for certified organic products. Farmer organizations are also eligible for pre-harvest credit.

Fair labor conditions: Workers on Fair Trade Certified farms enjoy freedom of association, safe working conditions, and fair wages. Forced child labor is strictly prohibited.

Direct trade: Importers purchase from Fair Trade producer groups as directly as possible, eliminating unnecessary middlemen and empowering farmers to develop the business capacity necessary to compete in the global marketplace.

Democratic and transparent organizations: Fair Trade farmers and farm workers decide democratically how to invest Fair Trade revenues, and proof of a democratic process is required.

Community development: Fair Trade farmers and farm workers invest Fair Trade premiums in social and business development projects like scholarship programs, quality improvement trainings, and organic certification.

Environmental sustainability: Harmful agrochemicals and GMOs (genetically modified organisms) are strictly prohibited. Environmentally sustainable farming methods are promoted that protect farmers' health and preserve valuable ecosystems for future generations, with the strictest prohibited materials list of any product certification, short of organic. Fair Trade farmers also protect the land and wildlife habitat by intercropping plant species to improve soil fertility and protect against erosion. FLO released new standards in January 2006, adding a stringent environmental management program that includes impact and monitoring, water and soil conservation, proper waste disposal, and prohibitions on planting in protected areas.

WHEN DID STARBUCKS BEGIN PURCHASING FAIR TRADE CERTIFIED COFFEE?

Starbucks introduced Fair Trade Certified coffee into its product line on October 4, 2000. In 2000, Starbucks purchased 190,000 pounds of Fair Trade Certified coffee.

HOW MUCH FAIR TRADE CERTIFIED COFFEE DOES STARBUCKS PURCHASE EACH YEAR?

Starbucks has steadily increased its purchases of Fair Trade Certified coffee each year, and it will double its 2009 purchases to 40 million pounds, making the company the largest purchaser of Fair Trade Certified coffee in the world.

Access to Credit

As previously stated, Starbucks is involved in providing funds so that coffee farmers can access credit. This allows them to receive assistance through times of cash shortages and during crop cycles. To date, Starbucks has given affordable credit to nearly 74,000 small farmers and suppliers. The company has committed $10.5 million to three not-for-profit organizations, including the Calvert Foundation. Shari Berenbach, president and CEO of the Calvert Foundation, talked about community investing and Starbucks' efforts to improve social and economic conditions for coffee farmers.

WHAT IS THE CALVERT FOUNDATION?

The name is Calvert Social Investment Foundation; we tend to call ourselves simply Calvert Foundation. We are a nonprofit 501(c) (3) organization launched by the Calvert Fund in 1995 in order to popularize investment as a tool to end poverty. We are engaged in channeling investment dollars to underserved communities.

HOW HAS STARBUCKS BEEN INVOLVED IN PROVIDING AFFORDABLE CREDIT TO FARMERS?

Through Starbucks' investment in Community Investment Notes, financing is provided to Farmers Cooperatives, which use the capital to provide post-harvesting financing. The chain begins with Starbucks investing with the Calvert Foundation, which in turn provides a cash loan to the cooperative, and the Farmers Cooperative is responsible for getting the cash to its members. This is an exciting and unique opportunity for many global farmers to get a fair price for their coffee. There is often a long delay between when the coffee is harvested and when it is cleaned, dried, and finally, sent out for shipment. The delay (which could be 12, 16, or 20 weeks) between harvesting and delivery of the coffee creates great hardship for the farmers. When farmers have access to credit, they are getting funds that are coming from the proceeds of the sale. Farmers often need capital to cover expenses for the next harvest. The reason it is so important is that some farmers may be hungry or sick and might otherwise need to turn to middlemen, coyotes, who will pay way below the fair market price. They may provide the farmers with only half of what they deserve.

Starbucks helps strengthen local cooperatives, which provide a range of services—loans, health care, schools, and social services—that better the lifestyle of farmers.

DO THE INVESTMENTS OF STARBUCKS SUPPORT FAIR TRADE COFFEE?

Starbucks' investment began in 2001. The company has two investments—one supporting Fair Trade and the other supporting domestic Community Development. The invested amount is fully targeted toward Fair Trade or intermediaries such as Root Capital, a nonprofit social investment fund that finances grassroots businesses in the developing world. These intermediaries then lend directly to other Fair Trade borrowers. Of Starbucks' total investment, nearly 66 percent is directed toward Fair Trade.

IN WHAT AREAS OF THE WORLD DO STARBUCKS INVESTMENTS POSITIVELY IMPACT COFFEE COMMUNITIES?

The investments we have collaborated in with Starbucks support Latin American coffee farmers, in particular those in Mexico, Nicaragua, and Costa Rica.

HOW DOES A LOAN DIFFER FROM CHARITY?

It differs in two ways. First, the funds are providing a sustainable financial strategy so that farmers may work their way out of poverty. A loan allows them access to credit, an opportunity many of us in the United States take for granted. Second, to the provider of financial resources, the investment is returned with interest. The Community Investment Notes offer investors an opportunity to earn a modest, yet reliable, 3 percent return.

YOU DECIDE

Setting the Price for a Cup of Coffee

The response of a consumer to a change in price is measured by an economic concept called *price elasticity of demand*. It is a numerical measure that helps explain people's behavior and a useful tool for economists, policymakers, or anyone making pricing decisions. The price elasticity of demand is measured by dividing the percentage change in quantity demanded by the percentage change in price. The mathematical measurement looks like this:

Price Elasticity (E) = % change in quantity demanded ÷ % change in price

Basic economics tells us that the quantity demanded will always go up when price moves down. Since price and quantity are inversely related, we know that price elasticity will always be negative. So we measure price elasticity as an absolute value and simply drop the negative sign. We know that when price rises, quantity demanded will fall. The question is—by how much? That is where you, as part of the technical team, come in.

Let's say you are the senior vice president of marketing for Carole's Comfortable Coffeehouse, and you're in charge of the annual product price review. It's a big job with the potential for a huge financial impact on the company's bottom line, so you'd better keep reading to brush up on your economics. What if the company reduced its price—would it sell so many more cups that revenue would burgeon? You must decide on a pricing strategy. But before making a decision, put on your economist's hat. We are going to explore the exciting worlds of *elasticity* and *inelasticity*.

Demand is elastic when the percentage change in price causes a greater percentage change in quantity demanded. If the absolute value of price elasticity is larger than 1, demand is elastic. Consumers respond significantly to a change in price. Big purchases like dishwashers, cars, and televisions tend to be sensitive to price changes and are elastic. Luxury goods, like diamonds or wine, have more elastic demand curves than necessity items. Also, goods with more substitutes have more elastic demand.

Let's look at an example. We'll assume that a store owner drops the price of a 36-inch-screen television by $50 for a holiday sale, from $450 to $400. The average price of the TV was $425. We can compute the percent of the change in price to see that the absolute value of the percentage change is $50 ÷ $425, or 0.118. The number sold of this specific model of 36-inch-screen TV went from 200 to 300 units. That means the average number of units sold was 250, so compute the percent change in quantity demanded as 100 ÷ 250—it rose by 40 percent. The price elasticity of demand would be 0.40 ÷ 0.118 = 3.39. This means that a 1 percent reduction in the price of the television triggers a 3.39 percent increase in purchases. The store owner can increase sales in a substantial manner by lowering the price.

Demand is inelastic when the percentage change in quantity demanded is less than the percentage change in price. If the absolute value of price elasticity is between 0 and 0.99, demand is inelastic. Necessity items, like coffee, prescription drugs, milk, and gasoline (over the short term) all tend to be relatively insensitive to a price change. Also, goods that amount to a relatively small percentage of your income, such as an apple, a pack of gum, or a pen, tend to be more inelastic.

For example, let us see what happens when a grocery store decides to run a huge sale on whole milk. The store manager drops the price of a gallon of whole milk from $4 to $3 in an effort to bring more people into her grocery store. The average price of a gallon of milk is $3.50. We can compute the percent change in price to see the absolute value of the percentage change as $1 ÷ $3.50 = 0.29. More gallons of milk will be sold, going from 10 to 11. So we'll compute the percent change in quantity demanded as 1 ÷ 10.5 = 0.10. The measurement is inelastic at 0.10 ÷ 0.29 = 0.34. This says that a 1 percent price reduction in milk triggers only a 0.34 percent increase in purchases. The store manager did not increase sales in a substantial manner by lowering the price; in fact, a change in price has relatively little effect on quantity demanded.

As you might imagine, the effect of a price change on total revenue depends on price elasticity. *Total revenue* is the amount of money received from product sales. That is, price × quantity = total revenue. Suppose we go back to the TV example. At $450 per TV, 200 units were sold, and total revenue was $90,000. When we lowered the price to $400, a total of 300 units were sold, and total revenue increased to $120,000. If demand is elastic, a price cut will increase total revenue. Conversely, an increase in price will mean lower total revenue. For a product with elastic demand, price and total revenue are inversely related. In this case, discounting the TVs was a fabulous move on the part of the store owner.

When demand is inelastic, a price cut will decrease total revenue. Conversely, a price hike will raise total revenue. For inelastic demand, then, price and total revenue are directly related. At $4 a gallon, 10 gallons of whole milk are sold, and the total revenue for milk sales equals $40. With a price reduction to $3, only 1 more gallon is sold, and at $3 times 11, the total revenue fell to just $33. This would not be a good move for the store manager.

So, here is your job assignment and dilemma as the senior VP for marketing at Carole's Comfortable Coffeehouse. Your economic projections state the following: The coffee price is set at $2 a cup, and daily sales are 200 brews a day. You are considering a rate increase to $2.50, and daily sales are projected to fall to 195 cups. Is this a wise move, based on total revenue projections? It looks like a good bet, but plug the numbers in for total revenue and price elasticity to make sure.

You get a cup of coffee and start working on the annual price review. A quick check of the calculator says this looks like a winner. At $2 a cup and 200 cups, there is $400 total revenue. But a price of $2.50 multiplied by 195 cups equals a total revenue of $487.50. You wish all your decisions could be so easy and give the green flag on the price increase. Daily revenue is projected to go up a total of $87.50. Check out the numerical elasticity measurement and you can see it is inelastic, fairly insensitive to price change: The price will change a total of $0.50 ÷ $2.25 = 0.22. To compute the percent change in quantity demanded, it is 5 ÷ 197.50 = 0.03. The measurement is inelastic at 0.03 ÷ 0.22 = 0.14. This says a 1 percent increase in coffee prices triggers just a 0.14 percent fall in purchases.

Price elasticity can be used to determine whether loyal coffee drinkers are willing to spend more money on their beverage when the price is increased. The key is whether you know you have an inelastic demand;

then you would never want to lower the price, because total revenue would fall. The typical Starbucks consumer spends about $4 for every purchase. Every year, prices are raised a nickel. At what dollar point would you quit raising prices? Do you think enough people would pay for a $5 cup of coffee in order to raise the company's total revenue? What about $10 a cup? Starbucks clearly has a relatively inelastic demand for coffee today. But at what price will demand for coffee become relatively elastic?

Chapter Five

How Starbucks Moved Ahead of the Competition

Starbucks' steadfast drive to become the best coffee retailer has resulted in its being the biggest coffee retailer.
—John Moore, *Tribal Knowledge: Business Wisdom Brewed from the Grounds of Starbucks Corporate Culture* (2006)

Starbucks has great relationships with its partners and customers. It treats the coffee farmers honestly and fairly, and its accomplishments are mutually beneficial. The company has made major impacts on the communities it serves through support of community events, charitable programs, and volunteerism. But the key element that has skyrocketed Starbucks to be the exceptional company it is today is inventiveness. The company's originality sets the groundwork for its success in the future. Let's take a look at some of the innovative programs and initiatives that have carved out its unique niche as the world's number one specialty coffee retailer.

Coffee Talk

CUP OF JOE?

Picking up your morning coffee, you may have heard it or even used the phrase yourself: "I am going to pick up a cup of joe." According to legend, the term *cup of joe* is attributed to former U.S. Navy Secretary Josephus Daniels. After Daniels banned alcohol from Navy vessels in 1914, the soldiers grudgingly began to drink coffee, referring to it as a cup of Joe, or joe.

THE WORLD'S BEST COFFEE BEANS

When people think of Starbucks, they think of superior quality. Starbucks coffee is the most recognized coffee brand around the world, and millions of people in 47 countries know Starbucks as the world's finest coffee. The company purchases the best green beans (raw coffee beans that have not been roasted) in the world. The beans are the first step that differentiates this company from all others in the specialty coffee industry. Plus, it has developed exceptional expertise in the beans' roasting.

A well-thought-out plan for selecting only the finest coffee beans illustrates Starbucks' passion for buying and roasting top-quality coffee. Starbucks purchases roughly 2 percent of coffee grown around the world, and as you can see from Table 5.1, coffee production is big business worldwide. Global output of green coffee beans exceeds 7.7 million tons (130 million bags). Starbucks does not purchase the lower-quality robusta beans, despite the fact that these beans are cheaper. Finding the higher-quality arabica coffee beans, grown in distinct regions of the world, helps the company maintain its unique niche and has kept it ahead of its competition.

Coffee buyers for Starbucks travel to the coffee-growing areas of Latin America, Africa and Arabia, and the Asia-Pacific region to purchase the premium coffee beans they demand. The evaluation process for buying the coffee includes roasting samples of coffee and taste-testing. This is a process called *cupping*, in which the aroma and aspects of taste (acidity, body, and flavor) are measured. Have you ever seen someone at a fancy restaurant savoring a sample of wine by holding it in her mouth for a few seconds to evaluate the bouquet and flavor? That is similar to cupping, but in this case, the commodity is coffee, and the taste-testers are professionals. Only a very few of the tested coffee samples will make it to the Starbucks warehouses. While over 60 countries grow coffee, Starbucks has only purchased from a select group. In fiscal 2007, Starbucks coffee was grown in 25 countries—the majority in Guatemala, Colombia, and Indonesia.

The purchased coffee beans are then shipped fresh to one of five company roasting facilities. Starbucks roasters are experts at releasing

Table 5.1
Green Coffee Producers 2007 Production (measured in tons)

Country		
Brazil	2,178,246	
Colombia	710,000	F
Ethiopia	325,800	*
Indonesia	665,500	*
Vietnam	1,060,000	*
WORLD TOTAL	7,742,675	

* = Unofficial figure; F = FAO estimate
Source: Food and Agriculture Organization of the United Nations, FAOSTAT

the entire flavor of the beans and are skilled in creating the signature Starbucks dark-roast flavor. Once roasted, the coffee beans are utilized for Starbucks Coffee, as well as the company's other brands: Seattle's Best Coffee and Torrefazione Italia.

Starbucks is willing to pay top dollar for quality beans, too. For fiscal 2007, world arabica prices averaged roughly $1.14 per pound. This is the "C" Contract market price and is the worldwide trading reference utilized by coffee traders. In the same time period, Starbucks paid an average of $1.43 per pound for arabica coffee beans. Starbucks pays more than the "C" price to compensate coffee farmers for maintaining premium quality. And while the "C" price tends to fluctuate due to speculation and annual weather conditions, the price Starbucks pays for its coffee tends to be relatively stable. Starbucks buys its green coffee beans from exporters, farmers, farm cooperatives, and, on occasion, other importers (see Appendix B: The Futures of Coffee).

What Is Coffee Cupping?

Coffee cupping is a method of evaluating the aroma and taste of brewed coffee. It is generally employed by professionals in the trade to evaluate the quality of a coffee bean, but cupping can be practiced by anyone to get an understanding of different coffee regions. Cupping requires first sniffing the coffee, then drawing a sip of the coffee to the roof of the month so it spreads to the back of the tongue, and finally rolling the coffee around in the mouth to begin to identify distinctive flavors and where it was grown. Most people then spit out the coffee.

Ask yourself, "Is it a full-bodied coffee?" and "Does it taste bitter?" Use statements like "The aroma is fruity" or "What a spicy aroma," and you will fit right in with the pros. See if you can pick out the traits that are unique to coffees from different regions. What makes a coffee from Costa Rica different from an Ethiopian-grown coffee? Comparing and contrasting coffees allows you to develop an appreciation of different coffees and their specific tastes. And although cuppers, as they are called, definitely have a unique professional skill, personal opinion comes into play.

According to the Specialty Coffee Association of America (SCAA), a cupper generally looks at these six characteristics:

- Fragrance—the smell of beans after grinding
- Aroma—the smell of ground-up beans after they are steeped in water
- Taste—the flavor of the coffee
- Nose—the vapors released by the coffee in the mouth
- Aftertaste—the vapors and flavors that remain after swallowing
- Body—the feel of the coffee in the mouth

Why not try your hand at cupping? Coffee tasting can be an interesting experience, so go ahead and prepare a simple coffee cupping for your favorite adult coffee drinkers—parents, relatives, or family friends. You should have no trouble finding willing participants. Comparing various brewed coffees can help one decide which bean is most to one's liking.

Keep it simple and start with just a few coffee varieties. Be sure to brew the coffee fresh. The samples should be small, and two fresh cups should be available for each coffee. A large spoon helps in the tasting. And, of course, make sure you have written down descriptions of your coffees to share with the taste testers, aka the cuppers, when they are done picking their favorites. Provide evaluation forms for the individuals to write down descriptive comments about each coffee. To increase their coffee IQ, at the end of the cupping, you can reveal the descriptions of the coffees and let each participant guess the origin of the coffee brews. The adults may enjoy the experience so much, they will want to have a formal coffee tasting party for their friends. Over 50 percent of Americans consume coffee on a regular basis, so a coffee party is likely going to be a popular event. Check out Ted Lingle's *The Coffee Cupper's Handbook* (Specialty Coffee Association of Amerca, Third Edition, 2008) for details on the terms, references, and protocols of cupping procedures.

PRODUCT DIFFERENTIATION: MORE THAN THE COFFEE

The economic definition of *monopolistic competition* is a market structure in which many firms compete by selling a similar, but not identical, good or service. There are numerous firms in the industry in this market structure, and the barriers to entry into the market are low. In other words, the costs are relatively low to start up a coffeehouse, and many have attempted to enter the market. Once people see an opportunity to make money, such as the coffeehouse phenomenon, many firms will enter the market in an attempt to make money. Many will fail, but some will succeed, and new entrants in the market will take some demand away from current producers in the market.

Starbucks is not a unique business; there are hundreds of firms running coffeehouses throughout the United States. The company's main long-time U.S. competitors are Caribou Coffee and, after that, Peet's Coffee & Tea. There are hundreds of smaller neighborhood coffee cafés, as well. But Starbucks' success has come from its expertise at product differentiation.

Starbucks has done a stellar job of taking an essentially similar retail good—coffee—and turning it into a unique product. The coffee, beverages, and food items that Starbucks sells are not identical to those at other coffeehouses. But, besides differentiating its consumable products, it has also created a priceless intangible product over the years that can't be duplicated by any other: the Starbucks Experience. Customers identify Starbucks with premium quality, serving the world's finest coffees in a friendly and welcoming setting. Starbucks coffeehouses also sell an elite dream, an atmosphere that can be a departure from real life, and a place for escape from the mundane.

Starbucks baristas boost this satisfying customer experience by adding education to each cup of coffee. By sharing information about the company's select coffees with purchasers—from the qualities that make their flavors unique to their countries of origin—baristas help Starbucks customers become more knowledgeable about what they are drinking, feel good about the product, and become a part of the Starbucks coffee culture. The company is promoting its coffee products the way winemakers have long marketed wines, making the type of grapes and the area where it was grown important to the product. Going to dinner and knowing which wine to order with your meal is impressive, and now the same can be said of Starbucks coffees.

Many competitors have tried to capitalize on the success of Starbucks and open their own upscale coffeehouses. Yet, the Starbucks Corporation has carved out such a unique package that it is impossible to fully duplicate. The company's retail coffeehouses become entwined with and support the communities in which they operate, and they develop a strong customer following. Starbucks customers are loyal and not likely to shift their preferences; each week, roughly 50 million people visit Starbucks to pay for pricey food and beverages. Starbucks has the power to raise prices without negative effect, because of great brand loyalty. It has brought the coffeehouse culture to life. When brandchannel. com's 2008 brandjunkie awards [sic] asked people "What brand can you not live without?" the results ranked Starbucks a powerful number five in the world.

THE STARBUCKS CARD

Research has shown the average person carries a total of four credit cards. Our wallets are bulging with plastic of all sorts—not only credit cards, but also gift cards, debit cards, and membership cards. Starbucks responded early on to the plastic phenomenon with a stored-value card program. In 2001, the company introduced the Starbucks Card, with gleaming success. Today, there are more than 160 million Starbucks Cards circulating. In fiscal 2007, the company hit $1 billion in sales being loaded on the cards and redeemed in a single year. As a stored-valued card program—load it up and then spend the money later— it makes buying simple for regular customers. It also reinforces customer loyalty by making them card-carrying members and more likely to pass by a competitor's store.

The Starbucks Web site, www.starbucks.com, provides details on this convenience card program. At the time of this writing, these were a few of the benefits offered when a customer uses a Starbucks Card for a purchase:

- Syrup and milk options on the house
- Free brewed-coffee refills
- A free 12-ounce beverage with each purchase of a pound of whole beans
- Two hours of free in-store Wi-Fi access per day

For those who frequent the coffeehouse on a regular basis, there is the Starbucks Gold card. It carries an annual membership fee, but the perks for the Starbucks lover are appealing. Details are available at www.star bucksgold.com, but the main benefit is a 10 percent discount on most purchases, excluding gift cards, publications, digital downloads, and member fees. For regulars, the discounts add up and can help ease wallet pain.

The card shows no signs of slowing down. The Starbucks Card has surpassed a total of $2.5 billion in total activations and reloads since its origination. And with such phenomenal success at home—in the United States and Canada—why stop? Mexico, Hong Kong, Australia, Thailand, Greece, and the United Kingdom are also part of the Starbucks Card global network. Japan, Taiwan, and Spain have Starbucks card programs that are unique to their markets.

Cool Cup Sizes

Think about the last time you went into a restaurant or a coffeehouse and ordered a drink. You might have ordered an extra large if you were super thirsty or wanted to savor a nice, hot beverage that would last awhile. A little java or just something quick to quench your thirst might have called for a small. Starbucks is definitely a trendy café, and it operates a cut above the mega fast-food establishments. Case in point—its cup sizes for hot and cold beverages. Hot beverages range from Short (8 fluid ounces) to Tall (12 fluid ounces), Grande (16 fluid ounces), and Venti (20 fluid ounces). Cold beverages range from Tall (12 fluid ounces) to Grande (16 fluid ounces) and Venti (24 fluid ounces). So you can go into a competitor and ask for a small coffee, or you can go into Starbucks and ask for a tall. You'd be served a 12-ounce cup in either place, but doesn't a *tall* sound so much cooler? That's Starbucks' marketing genius at work.

UNIQUE BEVERAGE AND MENU CHOICES

Starbucks carries over 30 varieties of blends and single-origination coffees, from mild to extra bold. Among the handcrafted beverages the store features are fresh-brewed coffees, hot and iced espresso beverages, coffee and noncoffee blended beverages, hot chocolates, and teas. Beverages are, so to speak, the meat and potatoes of the business; 75 percent of Starbucks' sales for company-operated stores result from beverages. Whole-bean coffee, food, and coffee- and tea-related merchandise account for the remaining 25 percent.

A host of related specialty merchandise is featured at the retail stores, including a line of premium chocolate, espresso machines, tumblers, mugs, coffee brewers, and coffee and tea items. In some retail markets, food items available may include a new health-oriented breakfast menu, pastries, sandwiches, and salads.

Each of Starbucks' 30-plus coffees has a distinctive flavor. This is just one of the ways the company has moved ahead of its competition—by having a flavor that's appealing to everyone. You can tell a lot about each coffee according to where it was grown. There are three growing regions that represent the source of all arabica coffee beans, and coffee from each region has a distinct flavor, unique to the area where it originates. Customers can further refine their favorite coffee niche by deciding if they favor mild, medium, bold, or extra bold roasts.

Coffee Talk

RECIPE FOR THE PERFECT CUP OF COFFEE

How do you brew the best cup of joe? Popular guidelines state that 2 tablespoons of ground coffee should be used per 6 ounces of water for a great cup of coffee. But you may choose to adjust the proportion of coffee up or down to suit your own particular preference in your quest for the perfect-tasting cup of coffee.

Starbucks has specific coffees from roughly 10 to 15 different countries, and each of these coffees has unique flavor characteristics. These are referred to within the company as *single-origin* coffees. Blends, on the other hand, bring together coffees from different areas, or origins, to create a different taste experience. Some coffees are purchased solely for blending, while others are purchased as single-origin offerings. Blending permits some unique taste variations.

Coffees from Latin America typically carry the flavors of soft spice, nuts, and cocoa. Central and South America top world coffee production; they produce more than any other growing region. These coffees have consistent quality and are fabulous for blending. Single-origin coffees by Starbucks typically come from the countries of Mexico, Guatemala, Costa Rica, Panama, and Colombia. One example is Organic Shade-Grown Mexico. This coffee, with a slightly nutty taste, comes from a multitude of small farms in the Southern Mexican state of Chiapas.

Coffees from the Africa and Arabia region are known for their berry-like and citrusy flavors. Favorites in this area include coffees from Ethiopia, Yemen, and Kenya. An example from this region is Kenya Coffee. This coffee is definitely fruity flavored and may remind you of berries or grapefruit.

Coffees from the Asia-Pacific region are bold, with earthy, herbal, or spicy flavors. An example is Decaf Sumatra Coffee. Sumatra, by the way, is the sixth-largest island in the world and is home to Mount Kerinci, a 12,467-foot peak. Decaf Sumatra may be a decaffeinated coffee, but it has an intense flavor, with an earthy undertone.

The company is also noted for its blended coffees. The most flavorful blend is Gold Coast Blend Coffee. This blend was created in 1987 to commemorate Starbucks' first store opening in Chicago. It is an extra bold coffee that showcases the best Latin American and Asian-Pacific coffees, accented with a hint of sweetness from Italian roast coffee.

Starbucks also markets its coffee through grocery stores and licenses its brand for other food and beverage products. Over the years, the company has created many successful coffee-related products, including a premium line of ready-to-drink beverages, coffee ice creams, and Starbucks liqueurs. Today, Starbucks coffee is available to customers in many grocery stores across North America and the United Kingdom. Chocolate, ice cream, and Frappuccino drinks are a hit in the grocery store market.

Starbucks ice cream is not new; it has been around since 1996. Check out your local grocery store for the delectable Starbucks ice creams. Talk

Starbucks coffee beans

about variety—the shopper can choose any one of four flavors. The ice cream is made with arabica coffee mixed with other flavors. The ice cream is not sold in Starbucks cafes, as most stores do not have freezers.

Starbucks is always thinking and always cutting-edge. Take a look at some of the recent innovations in Table 5.2. Don't the tasty concoctions sound great? Many probably sound familiar, which means you have already frequented one of the many Starbucks stores and had a taste. Have you tried the Pike Place Roast? This coffee, launched in April 2008, commemorates Starbucks' long heritage and expertise in buying, blending and roasting. Another cool bit of trivia is that its namesake is the Seattle Pike Place Market, the location of Starbucks' original store, where this tradition began. It is an everyday coffee brew with a milder taste than traditional Starbucks coffee, and it has opened to rave reviews.

If you are hot and need to cool off, check out the Vivanno Nourishing Blends; these are smoothies like no other. Vivanno was rolled out with two inviting flavors to choose from: the Orange Mango Banana Blend and the Banana Chocolate Blend. Tasty and healthy—each blend provides at least one serving of fruit (your mother will love that!) and is always less than 270 calories. For those who are health conscious, a Vivanno smoothie may just be a guilt-free indulgence.

Table 5.2
Starbucks Corporation New Innovations Beverage and Food Launch Dates, United States and Canada

October FY 2009

Salted Caramel Signature Hot Chocolate

Hazelnut Signature Hot Chocolate

Portobello Mushroom, Spinach, Feta, and Ricotta with Egg Piadini

Breakfast Sausage and Cheddar with Egg Piadini

November FY 2009

Espresso Truffle

Peppermint Mocha Twist

Gingersnap Latte

RTD [Ready to Drink]: IZZE Blackberry

Apple Cinnamon Stella

Caramel Macchiato Biscotti

Walker's Minty Chocolate Cookie

Source: www.starbucks.com

Each beverage can be customized, but the following are standard ingredients for both these yummy drinks:

- One whole banana
- Whey protein (16 grams) and fiber powder (5 grams)
- Ice
- Your choice of milk (2 percent is standard, but nonfat milk will cut off 20 calories and up to 3 grams of fat.)
- (Orange-Mango Naked Juice is always added in the Orange Mango Banana Blend)

Perhaps your mouth is watering by now? Mine is, too. But the point is that Starbucks stays ahead of the pack by responding to consumers' wishes. In this case, it's for something to go along with a healthier lifestyle. This is just one example of a company response to customer preferences for more healthy products—and an opportunity for Starbucks to build further loyalty and increase sales. Plain and simple—Starbucks responds to consumer demand in an effort to increase its sales. Scan the tasty items below to see what you have tried and what you would like to try.

EVERYBODY LOVES CHOCOLATE

You have likely heard the phrase, "everybody loves chocolate." While that might be a little too all-inclusive, there is definitely some truth to it. Most people do consider chocolate a fabulous treat. So, in 2008, Starbucks took hold of this thought and went chocolate wild. The company made two big announcements: the introduction of Starbucks-branded premium chocolates and Starbucks Signature Hot Chocolates.

Signing a deal in July 2007, Starbucks Coffee Company and The Hershey Company joined together and announced a development and distribution agreement to introduce a premium chocolate line. Hershey's is the expert—the largest North American manufacturer of quality chocolate and sugar confectionery products, with sales of nearly $5 billion a year. The Starbucks chocolates are created in partnership with Artisan Confections Company, a wholly owned subsidiary of The Hershey Company. Artisan Confections' unique portfolio contains some of the world's finest chocolate and specializes in the market of premium chocolate. This division of Hershey's includes Scharffen Berger, recognized for its high-cacao dark chocolate products, and Joseph Schmidt, celebrated for its chocolate truffles.

The following year, in 2008, the companies banded together to create an artisan-style chocolate infused with the flavors of Starbucks coffee, tea, and other authentic coffeehouse flavors. If there is one thing people like with their coffee, it is chocolate. The U.S. Department of Commerce Census Bureau reports that in 2006, the chocolate candy market had retail sales near $16 billion. Starbucks was smart to get in on this favorite American treat. A delectable duo, the treats are available at mass retail stores, grocers, and drug stores. Chocolates sell for $2.99 and up.

As described in a March 4, 2008, company press release, the collection includes signature dark, mocha, and milk chocolate bars and tasting squares; Tazo Chai, Passion, and Citron tea-infused chocolate tasting squares; Caffè Mocha, Chai, Espresso, Caramel Macchiato, and Madagascar Vanilla Bean Truffles; and Milk Chocolate–Covered Caffè Verona Coffee Beans. "Chocolate has always been a special part of the coffeehouse experience," said Wendy Piñero, vice president of consumer products for Starbucks Coffee Company. "We are excited to extend the Starbucks Experience into the world of premium chocolates with the same passion and care as we do our specialty coffees."

How about your chocolate in a cup? While the classic hot chocolate beverage has long been enjoyed at Starbucks, the company recently revved it up a notch. The new premium chocolate drinks are European-inspired beverages that, according to the company, "reinvent the drinkable chocolate category in the U.S." The drinks are richer, creamier, and less milk-based than standard North American hot chocolate. The new product is a super-premium blend containing four types of cocoa from West Africa.

Starbucks is always thinking, innovating, and hoping Americans' chocolate love affair will be intensified—translating to bigger dollars. "Given Starbucks coffee heritage of roasting some of the finest coffees in the world, it made perfect sense for us to bring the same level of excellence to create an innovative cocoa blend that delivers an unmatched chocolate flavor," said Rob Grady, vice president of global beverages at Starbucks, in a September 30, 2008, news release ("New Starbucks Signature Hot Chocolate Debuts: Intensifying the Chocolate Experience with Gourmet Flavor"). "Inspired by the cafes of Europe, artisan chocolatiers, and influenced by customer suggestions, we're excited to introduce new Starbucks Signature Hot Chocolates as the perfect indulgence." The line centers on the signature hot chocolate, with options for salted caramel and hazelnut flavors.

Coffee Talk

According to data from the International Coffee Organization (ICO), it is estimated that 1.6 billion cups of coffee are consumed worldwide every day. That is an amazing statistic when you consider that as of late 2008, according to the International Programs Center at the U.S. Census Bureau, the entire population of the world was just over 6.7 billion people. The ICO's statistic equates to slightly less than 600 billion cups consumed every year. It is clear that coffee is a drink with worldwide appeal!

ONLINE COMMUNICATION

Effective communication is what it is all about in the fast-paced Internet world, and Starbucks is at the peak of the trend. Building relationships with customers builds brand loyalty and draws new and repeat customers. The company's Web site is a reflection of the business, and Starbucks has put its stamp of approval on Internet communication. It's one more tool that can be used to reach out to customers and increase the company's exposure.

Promoting products and services on the company Web site is one of the most effective means of advertising. At www.starbucks.com, old-time Starbucks fans, as well as prospective customers, will be impressed. A Web site is a fabulous online brand and sales channel, and Starbucks has left no stone unturned. The site is visually appealing, and the Internet reader can spend hours browsing the site. A page titled Our Coffee allows a customer to investigate, research, and discover his favorite coffees. Our Stores will let the searcher find her favorite store based upon location and store perks. A section on the Starbucks Card displays cash rewards and Starbucks Gold promotions; At Home allows you to choose your favorite coffee blend; and For Business explains how other companies can bring one of the world's strongest brands into their businesses. For a trip down memory lane, go to About Us to investigate the origins of the company and check out the latest on Starbucks' philosophy regarding corporate and social responsibility. Customers can also choose to Shop Online and be directed to Starbucks Entertainment for music, books and movies; to a step-by-step process for customizing a Starbucks Card; or to the online Starbucks store at www.starbucksstore.com.

StarbucksStore.com is an alliance between Starbucks Coffee Company and Marina Del Rey–based Cooking.com. Cooking.com runs six different kitchen-related Web sites. The online Starbucks store allows customers to buy whole-bean and ground coffee, tea, and brewing equipment. The site provides descriptions of the flavorful taste of each coffee, together with information about the country or countries of origin and the characteristics of blends. Of course, Starbucks Cards can be purchased and reloaded there, too. Among other items, Starbucks lovers can find gift sets, mugs, tumblers, thermal bottles, syrups, sauces, and cocoas. At Starbucks, it is all about the customer, and online customers can also sign up for Starbucks At Home, the company's coffee subscription program, to have their favorite coffees, teas, and syrups reserved and shipped directly to them. Online account management is available, as well, so that a recurring subscription can be modified or shipments can be held when the subscriber is on vacation.

Starbucks deserves high marks for its interest in consumers and its openness to new ideas. In March 2008, Starbucks launched its first online suggestion site. Just go to www.mystarbucksidea.com to join this online community. It enables people to share their own suggestions and ideas, encouraging creativity and dialogue. Starbucks can act on the best ideas submitted, and the users can watch and see which suggestions the company will apply. You can share the ideas that matter to you and find out how they're putting those ideas to work. Look at Share Your Idea and View All Ideas on the Web site. And don't forget to submit your own vote for the idea you think is best; just remember that you will need to register to participate.

Make sure to look at Ideas Into Action, too, where customers can track the progress of the customer ideas Starbucks is working on implementing. The Starbucks employees who review the ideas and comments are called idea partners. There are more than 40 idea partners who are experts in their fields, such as coffee or community programs. They'll take a combination of the most popular and most original ideas and present them to company officials. Those that are the best fit will be chosen for implementation. Using this type of input and dialogue, consumers can help company leaders shape the future of Starbucks. The dialogue is extended beyond the coffeehouse. Not only does this engage more consumers, but it shows faith in customer ideas.

A Starbucks press release, dated March 19, 2008, ("Starbucks Unveils Stategic Initiatives to Transform and Innovate the Customer Experience") explained the customer-based endeavor:

This new community seeks to strengthen Starbucks' connection with customers by:

- Establishing a meaningful dialogue between and among community members and Starbucks, expanding the coffeehouse experience outside store walls;
- Creating a new space for customers to share ideas and be part of shaping Starbucks in the future; and
- Building an open forum to share the Starbucks story in a way that fosters authenticity, transparency, and leadership in conversations about Starbucks.

HIGH-SPEED INTERNET ACCESS

Wireless Internet access, or wireless fidelity (Wi-Fi), is now often standard fare in airports, malls, doctor's offices, hotels, restaurants, bookstores, and, of course, coffeehouses. This perk has come to be expected in certain types of businesses, and many other companies have provided wireless Internet service in an effort to attract people to their establishments. Starbucks is on the cutting edge of that group of coffeehouses who make surfing the net part of the daily routine for their customers. In fact, Internet access is available at more than 7,000 company-operated Starbucks stores across the United States.

Caribou Coffee is the second-largest company-owned specialty coffee-house operator in the world. It has 415 company-owned coffeehouses and 80 franchised locations and offers free Wi-Fi service for customers in more than 80 percent of its stores across the United States. Another substantial competitor is Peet's Coffee & Tea, which has just under 200 stores across the United States. Every one of its coffeehouses boasts free Wi-Fi service.

Just think about it—the longer a customer sits at a table in a coffee-house, the longer he is a captive audience for coffee and food sales. No matter if a customer is working, creating, studying, or just chatting online with friends and family, there are huge marketing advantages to offering wireless Internet access for customers. Starbucks has definitely picked up on this new trend. Accessing your laptop while sipping a hot cup of rich coffee is an in-store experience customers appreciate and will come back for. The customer experience is enhanced and customer loyalty is built even stronger.

Starbucks has a number of complimentary and paid Wi-Fi options available at most locations. Customers who buy a minimum $5 Starbucks Card and then register the card online receive two hours of free Wi-Fi service at any Starbucks location that offers Wi-Fi, courtesy of AT&T. The catch is simple—you need to use your card at least once a month and agree to receive up to four e-mails per year from AT&T. Better yet, if you're one of AT&T's 12 million DSL customers, you already qualify for free Wi-Fi at Starbucks. For everyone else, paid options are available. T-Mobile HotSpot customers can enjoy full Internet access at Starbucks stores through a roaming agreement between AT&T and T-Mobile. Customers can also buy and download music wirelessly to their iPhones, iPod Touches, or computer laptops via the iTunes Wi-Fi Music Store available at Starbucks.

COFFEE MASTER PROGRAM

Starbucks understands the importance of education and putting its partners' knowledge to good use. The Starbucks Coffee Master program was initiated at the turn of the decade. In the program, partners receive education in coffee brewing, tasting, and blends. If you notice someone behind the Starbucks counter in a black apron instead of green, that person has been awarded the certification of Coffee Master. A Coffee Master has been through a special program to learn about the growing and roasting aspects of the industry. Purchasing and fair-trade practices are also included. It is not an easy feat; partners must pass a series of tests following their training before they are named Coffee Masters.

Many of the personnel at Starbucks headquarters in Seattle are Coffee Masters, too. The education proponent has been a win-win for partners, customers, and Starbucks. Partners gain knowledge of coffee and the industry and a further fondness for the craft. Customers gain from their expertise and can ask the resident Coffee Master any questions they have about coffee. The program encourages partners to enter into dialogue with Starbucks customers and share their further coffee knowledge. And Starbucks wins, because happy partners and customers are both good for business. There are currently more than 25,000 Starbucks Coffee Masters in 27 countries.

HEALTH AND WELLNESS INITIATIVES

The health craze has hit the United States, and Starbucks has stepped up to answer the call for healthy alternatives. The growing demand for healthier foods and beverages has inspired Starbucks to produce a host of new products to choose from. Consumers have developed a fresh interest in the nutritional content of what they eat and drink, so Starbucks has responded by providing customers with a list of customization options. You can request that a beverage be made with nonfat milk, and don't forget—you don't need the tasty whipped cream on that delectable drink. The company now has a great selection of sugar-free syrups and sugar-free substitutes, too. Starbucks has taken its customers' comments about nutrition and calorie intake seriously, and it has responded by providing nutritional information for all its drinks and food choices in stores and on its Web site. It has even highlighted 20 different choices under 200 calories, like the tall brewed coffee at 5 calories and 0 grams of fat, or the tall nonfat cappuccino at 60 calories and 0 grams of fat.

In the latter part of 2008, Starbucks added six new breakfast options for customers to munch on—all healthy alternatives—while consuming their favorite coffee or other beverage. The new healthy breakfast items are a great start to the day, because they feature fewer calories and more protein and fiber. Check out the oatmeal, protein plate, whole-grain breakfast pastry, bran muffin, fruit-and-nut bar, and multigrain roll, all made from high-quality, wholesome ingredients.

Starbucks has listened to its customers' wishes over the years and keeps adding variety to its menu of foods and beverages. It has taken steps in recent years to increase the overall health factor of its offerings—keeping customers healthy makes good marketing sense, after all. Starbucks has removed all artificial trans fats from its foods and beverages in North America. Since 2007, the company has switched from whole milk to reduced-fat 2 percent milk as the standard for espresso-based drinks in all U.S. and Canadian company-operated stores. That means your beverage will be made with 2 percent milk unless you request otherwise. But, of course, customers can ask for whole, skim, or even soy milk. The company is also investigating reduced-fat options in markets outside of North America and anticipates a switch to reduced-fat milk in other countries where it is important for consumers and supply is available. These changes have caused core Starbucks beverages to decrease in overall calories by 14 percent, and standard bakery items have seen an average 5 percent decrease in calories. In the summer of 2008, Vivanno drinks were introduced—fruit smoothie blends with strong nutritional value. Current Vivanno options include Orange Mango Banana and Banana Chocolate. The company feels it is important to offer these healthier choices, while the more indulgent foods and beverages that customers love will also remain on the menu for a special treat.

Recipe

COFFEE-BANANA THICK SHAKE

INGREDIENTS:

1/4 cup brewed coffee (your choice), cooled to room temperature
2 cups vanilla ice cream
1/4 cup 2 percent milk
1 teaspoon vanilla extract
1 banana, sliced into small pieces

Instructions:

Mix all ingredients in a blender until shake thickens to desired consistency. Serves two.

Author's note: This is one of my very favorite milkshakes I like to create at home. It combines some fabulous foods—ice cream and bananas—with a great coffee. You can, of course, use any coffee in the shake, but I prefer Starbucks. It is particularly tasty on a hot summer day!

Coffee Industry Trends

Ted Lingle has an expansive wealth of knowledge about the coffee industry, with over 25 years of experience in the business. Since 2006, he has been the executive director of the Coffee Quality Institute (CQI), an organization he cofounded with the goal of creating a sustainable supply of quality coffee for the industry. Previously, Lingle served as executive director of the Specialty Coffee Association of America (SCAA). He is the author of *The Coffee Cupper's Handbook* (2008) and *The Coffee Brewing Handbook* (1996). Lingle was a founding cochairman of the SCAA and has also participated on committees for the National Coffee Association and National Coffee Service Association. In addition, he has served as chairman of the board of directors of the Coffee Development Group/Promotion Fund of the ICO. He was employed as vice president of marketing for Lingle Bros. Coffee, Inc., for 20 years. The coffee expert answered some pointed questions on coffee consumption, supply-and-demand instabilities, and industry trends:

WHAT IS THE COFFEE QUALITY INSTITUTE?

The Coffee Quality Institute (CQI) is a nonprofit association that was started 10 years ago. It is a 501(c)(3) foundation formed to improve the quality of coffee and the lives of the people that produce it. Much of our work is funded by USAID (U.S. Agency for International Development), our largest funding source.

HOW MUCH COFFEE IS CONSUMED WORLDWIDE EACH YEAR?

Coffee is the one of the most widely traded commodities in the world, with an industry employing over 120 million people worldwide. The world is currently consuming all the coffee it is producing. This comes to roughly 130 million bags of coffee a year. Each bag is 60 kilos, or 132 pounds.

HOW HAS PER CAPITA CONSUMPTION CHANGED OVER THE YEARS?

Per capita consumption in the United States went from 7 kilos per person to 3 kilos per person in a 30-year period, from 1962 to 1992. The primary reason was that in the 1960s, there was a downturn in the blend quality from the major roasters. Roasters started using the cheaper robusta blends, indirectly driving consumption down. Robusta has double the caffeine and a more bitter taste. Consumers responded appropriately by migrating to other beverages. (See Table 5.3 for more recent per capita consumption trends.)

Table 5.3
Per Capita Consumption of Coffee in Selected Importing Countries (in kilograms)

	2005	2006	2007
Canada	5.20	5.71	6.45
Finland	12.60	11.94	12.01
France	4.71	5.16	5.47
Germany	6.29	6.64	6.27
Italy	5.68	5.71	5.91
United Kingdom	2.67	3.03	2.79
Japan	3.34	3.41	3.41
Russian Federation	1.34	1.37	1.71
Switzerland	8.89	7.51	7.93
United States	**4.20**	**4.09**	**4.13**

Source: International Coffee Organization

HOW HAS THE GROWTH OF COFFEEHOUSES CHANGED COFFEE HABITS?

The trend started in the early 1960s that caused a paradigm shift. During that time, consumers began to realize there were major quality and taste differences in coffees. It changed their attitudes and behavior when it came to coffee purchasing. Consumers who would pay $4 for a pound of Folgers became comfortable paying $15 for a pound of Starbucks.

HOW DO DEMAND AND SUPPLY INSTABILITIES AFFECT THE PRICE OF COFFEE?

Beginning in the 1990s, a new country—Vietnam—jumped into the coffee market. While initially Vietnam produced 500,000 bags a year, in 2000, it was up to 15 million bags. Vietnam is now the second-leading coffee-producing country (after Brazil), producing a low-grade robusta. The prices were so low that many roasters have moved from higher-quality Central American arabica coffee to purchase from Vietnam.

But the market is really a two-tiered market based on quality. People can perceive quality taste differences, and caffeine content causes consumers to self-regulate. Robusta contains twice the caffeine of arabica, causing those who don't easily metabolize caffeine to reduce consumption. The lower-quality robusta coffees will continue to have lower prices due to increases in supply.

WHAT TYPE OF IMPACT HAS STARBUCKS MADE ON THE COFFEE INDUSTRY?

The industry was alive and well before Starbucks. The individuals who started Starbucks learned from Alfred Peet. He was one of those individuals who were learning the specialty coffee market in the 1960s and helped create the explosion for the market in the 1990s.

Starbucks was in the right place at the right time. Starbucks was one of the darlings of the 1990s, with a highly successfully initial public offering (IPO). Starbucks has brought high visibility to the consumer. It has dramatically expanded convenience reach for the consumer, making coffee a beverage of choice. It is no longer "Do I want a cup of coffee?" but "What kind of coffee do I want? An espresso, latté, or chilled cappuccino?"

Starbucks represents only one in four coffee stores, and one-half of the stores are independent businesses. Specialty coffee represents a business opportunity for an entrepreneur to risk it all and to take a chance to open the doors to a great business. It is the entrepreneurial sprit that drives Americans to start a business. The coffeehouse is a great model.

Converting Kilos to Pounds

If you need a little help reading the chart on per capita coffee consumption, let's take a moment for a quick math review on conversion. Here are the basic comparisons:

pounds ÷ 2.2 = kilograms
kilograms × 2.2 = pounds

As an example, look at the per-person coffee consumption in the U.S. for 2007—4.13 kilograms. That means each person (on average) consumed 9.09 pounds of coffee that year (4.13 kilograms × 2.2 = 9.09 pounds).

Pivotal Places

Think you know a lot about the global coffee company? Match the place to the sentence that is important in Starbucks history:

Choices:

Pike Place Market; Seattle; Japan; China; Milan

1. Starbucks made its first endeavor into international literacy by supporting educational programs in this country: _____
2. Starbucks' first international store was located in this country: _____
3. The original Starbucks store was located here: _____
4. Corporate headquarters and founding city of Starbucks: _____
5. After a business trip to this city, Howard Schultz was convinced the espresso café concept would be successful for Starbucks: _____

Answers: 1. China; 2. Japan; 3. Pike Place Market; 4. Seattle; 5. Milan

---

YOU DECIDE

Should Everything Be Nutritionally Friendly?

How about whole milk in a tall Salted Caramel Signature Hot Chocolate with whipped cream, which totals 500 calories and 26 grams of fat? Choosing skim milk in that Salted Caramel Signature Hot Chocolate and no whip brings it down to 420 calories and 18 grams of fat? Or maybe you crave a tall, whole-milk Double Chocolaty Chip Frappuccino Blended Crème with whip, at 300 calories and 14 grams of fat? They are all delicious, of course, but is it the responsibility of Starbucks executives to watch each customer's nutritional and caloric intake and provide only healthy options?

Obesity, defined as a body mass index (BMI) of 30 or greater, is a serious problem in the United States and worldwide. A recent study by the U.S. Centers for Disease Control and Prevention found that over 34 percent of American adults age 20 or older are obese. Obesity boosts the risk of many diseases and a host of other health problems. Is a retail company obligated to promote only healthful products and cut out less healthful choices? Starbucks provides consumer-friendly nutritional information that is easily accessible online and in its stores. Is that enough? Should customers be allowed to simply make their own nutritional choices?

One side of the debate says restaurants, cafes, and coffeehouses have an ethical obligation to use healthful ingredients when preparing food and drinks. Retail food establishments are ultimately serving the customers and should act in their best interests. Stores, therefore, should guide customer choice toward low-fat food choices.

Others say retail establishments should not make decisions about customer health. We live in a free society. Individuals have a choice if they want to consume a high-fat and high-calorie diet, a low-fat and minimum-calorie diet, or a balanced meal and beverage plan. It is the consumer's responsibility to become educated about nutrition and make proper nutritional decisions.

Chapter Six

Financial Results and Starbucks Leadership

Starbucks is a phenomenon. A very successful and surprising one.
—John Simmons, *My Sister's a Barista: How They Made
Starbucks a Home Away from Home* (2005)

WHAT IS A RECESSION?

Howard Schultz made mention of a "challenging economic environment" when reporting the fiscal 2008 earnings for Starbucks (News Release: "Starbucks Reports Fourth Quarter and Fiscal 2008 Results," November 10, 2008). Reading between the lines, he was talking about the recession the U.S. economy is experiencing as I write. And it's official—as of mid-2009, the United States is in a recession that economists say began in late 2007. Let's take a moment to examine what a recession is and who gets to decide if the economy has slowed down so much that a formal determination is made.

The agency that determines if the United States is in a recession is the National Bureau of Economic Research (NBER), a leading Cambridge, Massachusetts–based nonprofit economic research organization. A small group of highly esteemed economists, such as Chairman Robert Hall of Stanford University and Martin Feldstein of Harvard University, sit on the Business Cycle Dating Committee of the NBER, which makes recession and expansion calls. It is such an important body of economists that even the U.S. government adopts its calls. The function of the Business Cycle Dating Committee is to decide when the nation's economy has reached a peak (high point) or a trough (low point).

A *recession* is a prolonged period of time when a nation's economy is slowing down, or contracting. The Business Cycle Dating Committee explains the multitude of factors that influence a recession:

> Because a recession is a broad contraction of the economy, not confined to one sector, the committee emphasizes economy-wide measures of economic activity. The committee believes that domestic production and employment are the primary conceptual measures of economic activity. (Business Cycle Dating Committee, 2008)

Coffee Talk

According to Economic Research Service Food Availability Data
from the USDA, a reduction in regular coffee consumption in the
United States has transpired over the past 60 years. Annual U.S.
coffee consumption is less than half of what it was at its peak in
1946, at 46.42 gallons per person; compare that to 18.64 gallons per person in 2006. Why? Possibly because other options,
such as soft drinks and a host of nontraditional coffee options—
chilled cappuccinos, espressos, lattes—have permeated the coffee
culture.

Let me put it in plain language for you. During a recession, factory
production slows and unemployment rises. Personal income falls as
people lose their jobs or work fewer hours. Personal consumption de-
creases as consumers buy less of everything, particularly luxury items. So
a higher-priced gourmet coffee beverage for $4 may be forgone in lieu of
an inexpensive, $1 fast-food coffee. The stock market typically falters dur-
ing depressed economic times, too, including Starbucks' stock, which has
dipped downward.

The good news is that recessions tend to be relatively short-
lived. The average recession is 10 months long, and the typical expansion period, when economic activity booms, is 57 months long.
When the Business Cycle Dating Committee met via conference call
on November 28, 2008, the committee determined that a peak in economic activity had occurred in the U.S. economy in December 2007.
The peak marks the end of the expansion that began in November
2001 and the beginning of a recession. A recession begins when the
economy reaches a peak of activity and ends when the economy
reaches its trough. Between trough and peak, the economy is in an
expansion.

During this recession, homeowners have seen a substantial reduction in the value of their homes, and homes have become much harder
to sell, some sitting on the market without a sale for many months. The
recession has resulted in a depressed economic environment in virtually every business sector. But what was the origin of this recession?
The cause of the economic downturn in the United States was multifold, but one key factor has been the sub-prime problem. Plain and
simple, some financial institutions made mortgage loans to customers
who simply did not have the job security and financial wherewithal to
repay the loans. According to RealtyTrac, a leading online marketplace
for foreclosure properties based in Irvine, California, 1.84 percent of all
U.S. housing units received at least one foreclosure filing during 2008,
up from 1.03 percent in 2007.

Exacerbating the problem, these sub-prime mortgages were bundled up together into bonds and sold to major institutional investors around the globe—including insurance companies, pension funds, and huge financial institutions. These faltering investments with their resulting losses have crippled the financial markets both domestically and globally. The credit market is tight, and commercial bank lending has come to a screeching halt. With business activity down, naturally the unemployment rate has risen, hitting 9.4 percent in May 2009. The economic crisis is widespread.

Coffee Quiz

Guess which famous person owns nearly 3 percent of Starbucks:

   a. Oprah Winfrey
   b. President Obama
   c. Howard Schultz
   d. Jennifer Aniston

If you guessed C, you are correct. After reading this far, hopefully you got that one right! According to *Forbes'* CEO 2008 Compensation, Starbucks CEO Howard Schultz owns 2.44 percent of the global coffee giant. This was worth a staggering $311.3 million in early 2009 and is a sure sign that the coffee guru believes strongly in the company's successful future.

STARBUCKS' FINANCIAL PICTURE

The fiscal 2008 10-K report from Starbucks—a comprehensive summary of the company's performance—included very blunt words about the recessionary effects on its business:

> As a retailer that is dependent upon consumer discretionary spending, the Company will face an extremely challenging fiscal 2009 because Starbucks customers may have less money for discretionary purchases as a result of job losses, foreclosures, bankruptcies, reduced access to credit, and sharply falling home prices (Starbucks Corporation Form 10-K, 2008, p. 16).

Keep in mind that the economic downturn is the backdrop Starbucks is operating against when we look at its recent financial picture in this chapter and learn of company plans for the upcoming years. Schultz returned to the helm of Starbucks Corporation in January 2008 to lead the company in its major restructuring initiative and recessionary repositioning. Recently, the global retailer has seen declining U.S. store traffic, rising milk prices, a depressed stock price, and faltering sales. Starbucks' job now is to learn to operate efficiently during an economic downturn. And the company is up to the challenge, addressing the difficult economic times head-on.

Starbucks has launched an extreme transitional strategy. By cutting costs and focusing on customer-based initiatives, the coffee company's goal is to cut $500 million in costs for fiscal 2009. How will it accomplish such a daunting task? This list tells a few of the steps that have already been initiated:

- Hundreds of underperforming stores have been closed.
- New store expansion has slowed down.
- Some funds allocated for U.S. stores were moved into international expansion.
- Thousands of jobs were cut.
- Training for partners was beefed up.
- A new selection of economical coffee-and-breakfast pairings was introduced.
- Some stores have stopped brewing decaf after noon to better control waste.
- New products, including the milder Pike Place Roast coffee, were introduced.
- The $45 million company jet was put up for sale.
- Rewards were added to the Starbucks Card.

This lists just a few items, but it's easy to see that Starbucks has taken major steps to rejuvenate its business.

Now, let's move ahead and examine the company's financials. It is important to examine the profitability and sales numbers over a trend period to get a better perspective on the impressive growth this company has seen overall. The key factor is that the company's fundamentals are sound. Quality arabica coffee—with over 30 varieties available—is a great product, and people will keep drinking coffee, along with tea and all the other wonderful specialty drinks. Consumers will continue to eat—this we know for sure. Starbucks plans to stay at the forefront of the food-and-beverage industry. The company has all the ingredients for long-term success in place—a quality product, a strong brand name, sound core financials, a top-notch management team, and a highly experienced big-business board of directors. In a company press release dated November 10, 2008, Starbucks reported financial results for the fourth quarter in fiscal 2008:

> As Starbucks moves from fiscal 2008, a year of significant transition for the company, it is well positioned to deliver in fiscal 2009 with the following foundational planks in place:

- A re-architected cost structure to allow for long-term operating margin expansion
- A healthier store portfolio achieved through closure of under-performing stores
- A stronger value and rewards platform, consistent with Starbucks premium brand
- A renewed emphasis and investment around coffee leadership
- A galvanized company with a common purpose

"With a re-architected cost structure at the close of fiscal 2008, we began the new fiscal year with a healthier store portfolio that will allow for operating margin expansion," commented Howard Schultz, chairman, president and CEO. "Despite a global economic environment which shows no immediate signs of improvement, the steps we took in FY08 position us to deliver EPS growth in FY09," Schultz noted further. "I am optimistic we are well positioned to weather this challenging economic environment."

As you can see from Table 6.1, Starbucks has assets valued at $5.7 billion dollars for fiscal 2008, an upward trend from $5.3 billion the previous year. This is a huge jump from the total asset value of $3.4 billion in fiscal 2004. Sales for the company increased to $10.4 billion in fiscal 2008, up from $9.4 billion a year earlier. Again, this is a substantial rise from the fiscal 2004 sales of $5.3 billion.

There are some grounds for concern, though. For fiscal 2008, the company reported a net income of $315.5 million, or $0.43 a share. This is a sharp downward dip from the $672.6 million, or $0.87 a share, one year earlier. Although profit margins (net profit divided by sales) remained in the 7 percent range for fiscal years 2004, 2005, 2006, and 2007, the margin dropped to 3 percent in 2008. Starbucks is not issuing a specific quarterly-earnings forecast for fiscal 2009. The margin compression was due primarily to relatively lower sales, along with restructuring changes associated with store closures and other transformational strategies. Despite cost-control efforts by the company, a drop in store traffic is expected to keep profit margins down. The company has generated strong cash flow from operating activities—$1.3 billion—which is essentially flat for fiscal 2008 and 2007, a huge positive. Note that the company took on $550 million of long-term debt in 2007, which will mature in 2017. The company no doubt took advantage of its strong name and borrowing ability to issue debt during a tough economy, perhaps in an effort to bring a boost to its stock price. Good news—the company has been generating the cash flow to cover the debt, has additional short-term borrowing capacity, and appears to have no liquidity problems.

Table 6.1
Starbucks: Key Financial Data for 2008

	Fiscal 2008 9/28/2008 (52 weeks)	Fiscal 2007 9/30/2007 (52 weeks)	Fiscal 2006 10/01/2006 (52 weeks)	Fiscal 2005 10/02/2005 (52 weeks)	Fiscal 2004 10/03/2004 (53 weeks)
Sales	$10.4 billion	$9.4 billion	$7.8 billion	$6.4 billion	$5.3 billion
Net Income	$315.5 million	$672.6 million	$564.3 million	$494.4 million	$388.9 million
Net Profit Margin	3.0 percent	7.1 percent	7.5 percent	7.8 percent	7.3 percent
EPS	$0.43	$0.87	$0.73	$0.61	$0.47
Long-term Debt	$550 million	$550 million	$2.0 million	$2.9 million	$3.6 million
Cash from Operating Activities	$1.3 billion	$1.3 billion	$1.1 billion	$923 million	$863 million
Total Assets	$5.7 billion	$5.3 billion	$4.4 billion	$3.5 billion	$3.4 billion

Source: Starbucks Corporation 10-K 2008

THE STORES

Starbucks is a big-time coffee retailer, and at the end of fiscal 2008, it had 16,680 stores (see Table 6.2). This is roughly double the total number of stores in fiscal 2004, at 8,569. The only words that can be used to describe this phenomenon are astronomical growth. But in July 2008, the company announced it would close approximately 600 U.S. stores and reduce the number of company-operated stores in Australia by 61; most of these closures were to be completed by mid-2009. These were mostly underperforming stores, with a few new locations that were still getting ready for business. California and Florida were the states hardest hit. Those areas had the most closures due to the depressed housing market and the credit crunch.

The positive spin from this news is that Starbucks began fiscal 2009 with a healthier group of stores. Future opportunities for the company's growth seem most likely to lie in the international operating segment. International operations generated roughly 20 percent of Starbucks' company-operated retail revenues in 2008. The company entered the international arena in 1996, and overall, its international operations are still in the early stages of development and require more support than its

Table 6.2
Starbucks Stores Open at Year's End, Fiscal 2008

	Fiscal 2008	Fiscal 2007	Fiscal 2006	Fiscal 2005	Fiscal 2004
U.S. Stores	11,567	10,684	8,896	7,353	6,177
International Stores	5,113	4,327	3,544	2,888	2,392
Total Stores	16,680	15,011	12,440	10,241	8,569

Source: Starbucks Corporation 10-K 2008

U.S. stores. This continued investment is part of the company's long-term plan for profitable growth.

LESSONS LEARNED

Just as individuals and families are learning new lessons in budgeting and controlling credit in the recessionary months, so too is Starbucks. Starbucks will watch costs, critique expansion plans carefully, and make an effort to be more in tune with customer needs. The company will be a leaner, more efficiently run business when the economy rebounds.

EXECUTIVE TEAM

Executive officers are the top leaders of a corporation. This group is in charge of running a company on a daily basis. The chief executive officer (CEO) is the top position—the person in charge of the overall management of a company. Additionally, the CEO is responsible for reporting to the board of directors.

One huge advantage that Starbucks has is its skilled executive leadership. This top-notch team of execs is led by a man with a vision, Schultz, who is the president and CEO of the company, along with being board chairman. In 1982, Schultz joined Starbucks Coffee Company as director of retail operations and marketing. In 1987, along with a group of investors, he purchased Starbucks Coffee Company's six stores, and he has never looked back.

Schultz has received a multitude of awards and acknowledgements throughout his career. They reflect the success he has achieved in his quest to make the Starbucks Corporation into the world's largest specialty retailer of gourmet coffee. In 2004, Schultz was named to The Time 100, *Time* magazine's annual list of the most influential people in the world today. He was placed in the Builders and Titans category. Schultz's leadership style permeates the Starbucks culture. He is a strong director, a visionary, and is overwhelmingly credited for the success of Starbucks. A charismatic leader like Schultz inspires those around him to do great work, too. Schultz has always been alert and listened to what Starbucks customers want, and he has a spectacular vision for new beverage and food products. The proof is easy to see. Under Schultz's leadership, the six stores he purchased in 1987 have multiplied; in 2009, the store total was over 16,000.

In the following paragraphs, you will find biographical descriptions of the Starbucks senior executives taken from the company's Fiscal 2008 10-K, filed with the United States Securities and Exchange Commission, unless otherwise noted. As you will see, Schultz has a group of high-powered and experienced executive officers working with him. Schultz is a great leader, but he also directs a competent and talented executive team—by all accounts, an experienced team with a proven record at Starbucks and with other major companies worldwide. A skilled executive team is essential for the continued health of Starbucks, and this group looks to have the credentials to weather any economic storm.

Howard Schultz, 55, Chairman, President, and CEO

Howard Schultz is the founder of the new Starbucks and serves as the company's chairman, president, and CEO. Schultz has served as chairman of the board since the company's inception in 1985, and he resumed his role as president and CEO in January 2008. From June 2000 to February 2005, he held the title of chief global strategist. From November 1985 to June 2000, he served as CEO. From November 1985 to June 1994, Schultz also served as president.

Cliff Burrows, 44, President of Starbucks Coffee U.S.

Cliff Burrows joined Starbucks in April 2001 and has served as president of Starbucks Coffee U.S. since March 2008. He served as president for the company's Europe, Middle East, and Africa division from April 2006 to March 2008 and as vice president and managing director for the United Kingdom prior to April 2006. Prior to joining Starbucks, Burrows served in various management positions with Habitat Designs, Ltd., a furniture and housewares retailer.

Martin P. Coles, 53, President of Starbucks Coffee International

Martin P. Coles joined Starbucks in April 2004 as president of Starbucks Coffee International, and in July 2008, he reassumed this role after having served as chief operating officer from September 2007 to July 2008.

Prior to joining Starbucks, Coles was an executive vice president of Reebok International, Ltd., a sports and fitness products company, from December 2001 to February 2004. Coles had previously held several executive-level management sales and operations positions with NIKE, Inc., Letsbuyit. com, and Gateway, Inc.

John Culver, Executive Vice President; President of Global Consumer Products, Foodservice, and Seattle's Best Coffee

Culver, 48, has been a Starbucks partner (employee) since 2002 and has held leadership roles in the company's Foodservice and Starbucks Coffee International business units. As the vice president and general manager of food service, he was responsible for leading its sales, marketing and operations. Most recently, he was responsible for cultivating the Starbucks Experience for all Starbucks company-operated, joint-venture, and licensed markets within the Asia-Pacific region.

- A Starbucks Corporation press release dated February 9, 2009, announced Culver's present appointment as of February 20, 2009.

Arthur Rubinfeld, 55, President of Global Development

Arthur Rubinfeld rejoined Starbucks in February 2008 as president of global development. Rubinfeld also serves as president of Airvision LLC, an advisory firm specializing in brand positioning that he founded in June 2002. From March 2006 to February 2008, he served as executive vice president of corporate strategy and chief development officer at Potbelly Sandwich Works. Prior to 2002, Rubinfeld held several positions in store development at Starbucks.

Troy Alstead, 45, Executive Vice President, Chief Financial Officer, and Chief Administrative Officer

Troy Alstead joined Starbucks in 1992 and currently serves as the company's executive vice president, chief financial officer, and chief administrative officer of global finance, a position he has held since the end of November 2008. Alstead previously served as senior vice president of global finance beginning in September 2007; as chief operating officer of Starbucks Greater China from April 2008 to September 2008; as senior vice president of corporate finance from September 2004 to August 2007; as interim president of Starbucks Europe, Middle East, and Africa from April 2003 through August 2004; and as senior vice president of Starbucks Coffee International from March 2003 through March 2004. Alstead served in a number of other senior positions with Starbucks prior to 2004.

Paula E. Boggs, 49, Executive Vice President, General Counsel, and Secretary

Paula E. Boggs joined Starbucks in September 2002 as executive vice president, general counsel, and secretary. Prior to joining Starbucks, she served as vice president legal for products, operations, and information technology at Dell Computer Corporation from 1997 to 2002. From 1995 to 1997, Boggs was a partner with the law firm of Preston Gates & Ellis (now K&L Gates). She served in several roles at the Pentagon, White House, and U.S. Department of Justice between 1984 and 1995.

Michelle Gass, 40, Executive Vice President of Marketing and Category

Michelle Gass joined Starbucks in 1996 and assumed the role of executive vice president of marketing and category beginning December 1, 2008. Gass previously served as senior vice president of marketing and category since July 2008; as senior vice president of global strategy, office of the CEO, from January 2008 to July 2008; as senior vice president of global product and brand from August 2007 to January 2008; as senior vice president of U.S. category management from May 2004 to August 2007; and as vice president of U.S. category management from October 2003 to April 2004. She served in a number of other positions with Starbucks prior to 2003.

Peter D. Gibbons, 47, Executive Vice President of Global Supply Chain Operations

Peter D. Gibbons joined Starbucks in February 2007 and has served as executive vice president of global supply chain operations since July 2008. From February 2007 to July 2008, Gibbons was senior vice president of global manufacturing operations. From March 1999 to February 2007, he was executive vice president, supply chain, of The Glidden Company, a subsidiary of ICI Americas, Inc.

Dorothy J. Kim, 46, Executive Vice President, Global Strategy, Office of the CEO

Dorothy J. Kim joined Starbucks in November 1995 and has served as executive vice president global strategy, office of the CEO, since July 2008. From December 2004 to July 2008, Kim served as executive vice president of supply chain operations. From April 2003 to December 2004, she served as senior vice president of global logistics, planning and procurement. Prior to April 2003, she served in various executive roles in supply chain and coffee operations and also held several positions in retail planning and operations.

Olden Lee, 66, Interim Executive Vice President, Partner Resources

Lee has been a director on Starbucks' board since 2003. Lee worked for PepsiCo, Inc., for 28 years in a variety of positions, including senior vice president of human resources for Taco Bell and senior vice president and chief personnel officer of the KFC division. Lee is also founder and principal of Lee Management Consulting, a management consulting firm.

- A Starbucks Corporation press release dated April 6, 2009, announced this interim appointment beginning immediately.

BOARD OF DIRECTORS

A board of directors is made up of individuals elected by shareholders of a business who have ultimate governing authority. These individuals make decisions for the company on behalf of the owners. In general, it is the board's job to take care of the big business decisions, such as establishing corporate management policies, appointing senior management, approving executive compensation, determining dividend and options policies, and deciding if a merger or acquisition would be advantageous for the company.

The Starbucks board of directors has adopted governance principles and committee charters to lead the company. The Starbucks Corporate Governance Principles and Practices for the Board of Directors read as follows:

> The fundamental responsibility of the company's board of directors is to promote the best interests of the company and its shareholders by overseeing the management of the company's business affairs. In doing so, board members have two basic legal obligations to the company and its shareholders: (1) the duty of care, which generally requires that board members exercise appropriate diligence in making decisions and in overseeing management of the company; and (2) the duty of loyalty, which generally requires that board members make decisions based on the best interests of the company and its shareholders, without regard to personal interest.

Members of a board usually include senior executives from the company, who are called *inside directors*. Schultz, for example, sits on the board and serves as its chairman. *Outside directors*, as the other board members are called, are highly respected individuals from the community. As of this writing, Starbucks had 11 top players. Up to 12 members may sit on the board. According to the Starbucks Corporate Governance Principles and Practices, "the board shall meet at least five times during the fiscal year, and may hold more meetings if necessary or appropriate."

Let's take a look at the high-level group of individuals governing this organization: the Starbucks Corporation Board of Directors. You will see the expansive breadth of big-business leadership these individuals bring to the table. Also notably, many members carry longevity of service on the board, lending insightful expertise to ensure the continued success of the Starbucks mission.

The Starbucks board members represent a variety of perspectives and skills from the group's stellar business and professional experience. Notice—you won't find anyone over age 70 on the board. There is mandatory retirement immediately before the company's annual meeting during the calendar year when a board member turns 70. This is done in an effort to keep professionals on the board who are in tune with the work environment of today.

STARBUCKS CORPORATION BOARD OF DIRECTORS

Howard Schultz, Starbucks founder, chairman, president, and CEO

Schultz, 55, has served as chairman of the board since its inception in 1985.

Barbara Bass, Gerson Bakar Foundation, president

Bass, 56, has been a Starbucks director since January 1996.

William W. Bradley, Allen & Company, LLC, managing director

Bradley, 64, has been a Starbucks director since June 2003.

Mellody Hobson, Ariel Capital Management, LLC, Ariel Mutual Funds, president

Hobson, 38, has been a Starbucks director since February 2005.

Kevin R. Johnson, Juniper Networks, Inc., chief executive officer

Johnson, 48, has been a Starbucks director since March 2009.

Olden Lee, Starbucks, interim executive vice president, partner resources

Lee, 66, has been a Starbucks director since June 2003.

Sheryl Sandberg, Facebook, Inc., chief operating officer

Sandberg, 39, has been a Starbucks director since March 2009.

James G. Shennan, Jr., Trinity Ventures, general partner emeritus

Shennan, 66, has been a Starbucks director since March 1990.

Javier G. Teruel, Colgate-Palmolive Company, retired vice chairman

Teruel, 57, has been a Starbucks director since September 2005.

Myron E. Ullman, III, J.C. Penney Company, Inc., chairman and CEO

Ullman, 61, has been a Starbucks director since January 2003.

Craig E. Weatherup, Pepsi-Cola Company, retired CEO

Weatherup, 62, has been a Starbucks director since February 1999.

ANNUAL STOCKHOLDERS MEETINGS

Annual meetings are important events, because they represent an annual review of a company's performance and provide insight into future business activities. This keeps stockholders abreast of future plans and allows them to vote on important company actions, such as electing new members to the board of directors. Starbucks' annual meetings are ticketed events open to all shareholders and are highly anticipated extravaganzas. Musician K.D. Lang performed onstage for stockholders at the 2008 meeting, and Starbucks employees were there to hand out gift bags filled with coffee goodies to shareholders as they left the affair.

The 2008 annual meeting was held March 19, 2008, when over 6,000 shareholders gathered at McCaw Hall (Seattle's opera house) at Seattle Center. They went to listen to Starbucks leader Schultz, newly reinstated as CEO, review the financials and unveil the company's new initiatives to revitalize the business. A company press release dated March 19, 2008, explains:

At the Annual Meeting, Starbucks unveiled the following new initiatives. They are focused on improving the current state of the U.S. business, re-igniting the emotional attachment with customers, and making foundational changes for the long term:

- A proprietary and revolutionary in-store Clover® brewing system that delivers the best cup of brewed coffee available anywhere;
- A complete reinvention of brewed coffee in-store that will be brought to life by baristas across the United States, who will scoop and grind a new unique coffee blend, connecting customers to the early days of Starbucks;
- The introduction of a new state-of-the-art espresso system that provides the perfect shot every time and helps facilitate the critical connection between barista and customer;
- The first phase of a Starbucks Card Rewards program, rewarding registered cardholders and providing unique new benefits when using their cards in Starbucks stores;
- The launch of MyStarbucksIdea.com, Starbucks first online community, that takes the Starbucks Experience outside the store and enables customers to play a role in shaping the company's future; and,
- An expanded relationship with Conservation International that enhances Starbucks' 37-year commitment to ethically sourcing the world's finest coffees and reaffirms Starbucks' leadership position in sustainable sourcing and climate preservation.

Here's the quick lowdown on various company actions that were announced:

The Clover. Starbucks announced that it would purchase The Coffee Equipment Company, which makes the Clover brewing system. Similar to a French coffee press, but with a special vacuum technology, this expensive piece of equipment produces superior brewed coffee and will be rolled out in select U.S. and international stores.

A new blend—Pike Place Roast. Named after the first Starbucks location, Pike Place Roast is a milder coffee, smooth and bold, that is now served every day in all of the company-operated U.S. stores, providing a fresh-brewed experience.

Next-generation espresso machines. Starbucks will install high-tech espresso machines in all U.S. stores. The Masterna, a state-of-the-art espresso machine, is shorter than the previous model used and saves employees some work, because it grinds coffee beans freshly as needed. The compact size of the new machine allows baristas to interact with customers as they are making drinks. The machine is scheduled to be in 75 percent of U.S. stores by late 2010.

An online networking site. At www.mystarbucksidea.com, customers can have a say in the company's future plans. Monitored by Starbucks partners, customers can submit their ideas and suggestions for the company and then track the progress of the top ideas as Starbucks works to bring them to life.

Adding rewards to the Starbucks card. Value-added benefits— like two hours of free in-store Wi-Fi and free refills on brewed coffee— are awarded to Starbucks Card holders.

Expanding Starbucks' commitment to Conservation International (CI). Starbucks has expanded its decade-long relationship with CI with a five-year global commitment to combat climate change.

The highly anticipated 2009 annual meeting followed on March 18, 2009, also in McCaw Hall at Seattle Center. In attendance was a small crowd of roughly 1,200 shareholders, likely because the meeting was available online for the first time, both as a live Webcast and in replay for a month after the meeting.

A detailed press release from the company, with a summary of the annual meeting, was released that same day. The CEO reassured stockholders that the company is financially strong. "Despite the challenging economic environment, Starbucks is profitable, has a strong balance sheet and generates solid cash from operations," Schultz was quoted as saying. He also noted that "trust in the Starbucks brand remains at a high level. We are laser-focused on delivering the finest-quality coffee and getting the customer experience right every time."

Starbucks Experiments with $1 Coffee

Starbucks is not afraid to try new things. On January 23, 2008, *The Wall Street Journal* reported that Starbucks was testing a $1 cup of coffee, as well as free refills on some brews, as part of a trial run in Seattle. That is about 50 cents less than what the short brew would regularly sell for, although prices can vary from store to store. An eight-ounce short brew at the test price rivals even McDonald's and Dunkin' Donuts, companies that have heaped some heavy competition on the global coffee giant as of late. Both of these fierce fast-food competitors start their coffee prices in the low- to mid-$1 range.

The initiative has apparently created some buzz. In a Starbucks transformation agenda press release (January 30, 2008), Schultz commented, "We have received a lot of attention in the last week about the $1 brewed coffee 8-ounce short test. Testing is a way of life for us as we continue to find ways to enhance the customer experience. Right now, as a test, it makes sense to us. I'd like to reiterate that Starbucks is built on premium coffee and a premium experience. We intend to maintain our leadership position at the high end, while broadening our appeal. And similar to other leading global consumer brands, we believe there are opportunities to create market segmentation, provide an entry point for new customers, and generate trial in a way that will also maintain the value of our core brand proposition."

It sounds as if we shouldn't count on the $1 Starbucks coffee becoming standard fare, but give the company an A+ for thinking outside the box. The short-term experiment was well received and created a great deal of excitement from customers. Testing, challenging assumptions, looking at a new perspective, and breaking the mold can all lead to creative new ways to build a business. Starbucks, with Schultz still at the helm, continues to dream and experiment with ways to better serve its customers.

YOU DECIDE

Sell the Jet?

You'll find no argument about whether Starbucks has been hit by the downturn in the economy. But while earnings have significantly faltered, the company still remains profitable. The management team is taking a head-on approach to keeping the company strong and viable. One of the tactics the company has seriously engaged in to remain a viable business is cutting costs. This means closing stores, cutting jobs, and yes, putting all three of the corporate jets up for sale.

In December 2008, Starbucks took delivery of its new Gulfstream 550—a $45 million jet. The company had placed the order three years earlier and would have been hit with huge fees for canceling the order. The Gulfstream 550 is a long-range aircraft and can accommodate up to 19 passengers. Three years prior, when the order was placed, the economy was in an expansion period and the company stock price was bolstered. The Starbucks jet is lightly used, to say the least, having made only 15 flights.

Even before the new plane was delivered, Starbucks had already placed its seven-year-old Gulfstream V up for sale. And according to a March 6, 2009, article in the *Seattle Times*, the company also wants to sell its third plane, a five-year-old Challenger 604 by Bombardier that accommodates 10.

Why have corporate jets? One side of the debate says executives are busy and it makes more sense economically to use a corporate jet. Their time is worth money. The private jet is, in a sense, an office where execs can work and exchange ideas. Commercial flights can be time wasting and often result in delays and cancellations. With a private jet, an executive can have a meeting on the opposite coast in the morning and be assured he'll be back the same day for a late-afternoon board meeting at headquarters. For Starbucks, which has over 16,000 stores in 46 countries outside the United States, the efficiency argument may be strong.

The other side of the coin says corporate jets are an excess—an extravagance useful only for the corporate ego. The millions of dollars devoted to the lavish travel style they represent are not a good use of corporate funds in good economic times or troubled. Executives can drive or take commercial flights when needed, or corporate jets can be leased.

The down economy has played hardball with the aviation market. Put on top of that the recent venting against corporate air travel and you have huge aircraft inventories and jet prices that have dropped by 30 percent or more because of the flood of used jets on the market. When CEOs from the Detroit 3 automakers flew into Washington, D.C., in private planes to testify before Congress in 2009, it caused quite an uproar. The ironic reason? While still enjoying luxurious private travel, the troubled automakers were there to discuss multibillion-dollar government loan assistance. While Ford did not seek short-term financial assistance from the government, GM and Chrysler did receive emergency funding. Likely in order to calm the extreme public relations debacle, GM and Ford announced they would sell their fleets of corporate jets. Chrysler leases its jets from an aircraft operator.

Financially scarred Citigroup has canceled its order for a new $50 million luxury corporate jet after the new Obama administration complained about the purchase. Citigroup has accepted $45 billion in taxpayer funds to help it through the recession. Bank of America, which also received $45 billion in government funds, took a close look at its travel accommodations, too. As part of a cost-reduction plan, the bank has announced it is scaling back its use of corporate aircraft and selling three jets from its fleet. Also up on the selling block is its Merrill Lynch helicopter, acquired from its recent purchase of the distressed brokerage. Not only is cost-cutting and image awareness hurting the aircraft sales market, but the group of potential buyers is also shrinking, because it is tough to get financing. Banks and financial institutions see aircraft as a risky venture to finance in today's market. Consider their viewpoint: In the event they had to repossess a plane, the market is already flooded. As businesses struggle, banks must more seriously evaluate the creditworthiness of a company.

What do you think? If you were the executive of a big company, would you make the same decision and place your fleet of planes up for sale? Do you think the executive staff will lose much efficiency by driving and having to take commercial airlines? If you were traveling across the United States and overseas on business, would you charter a private jet? Think about your plans and strategies for company travel.

Chapter Seven

Controversy and Coffee Competition

But Starbucks, with its coffee-centric culture and relentless visibility, has become a public icon; and its success, visibility, and self-ascribed probity invite scrutiny.
—Kim Fellner, *Wrestling with Starbucks: Conscience, Capital, and Cappuccino* (2008)

Starbucks has certainly had its share of troubles in recent years. The company saw its first-ever decline in store visits by consumers during the last quarter of 2007, its financial health is less robust than before, revenue has fallen off, and competition is percolating. It is struggling in the midst of an economic downturn to serve customers an escape from reality, along with a gourmet roast or other tasty treat. On top of this, the company has suffered from some criticism and bad press recently. Some of the less flattering critiques claim the company employs an anticompetitive strategy; it doesn't play fair with employee rights; it is cashing in on a supposed humanitarian cause; and, a sore point for the environmentally concerned, its paper cups are not recyclable. Let us explore and get to the root of these rumors.

CONTROVERSY 101: THE MOM-AND-POP CAFES BROUHAHA

Okay, let's just say it, because it is the elephant in the room. No doubt you have heard it before: Starbucks puts small, mom-and-pop coffeehouses out of business. Critics argue that the global coffeehouse doesn't play fair. They maintain that the coffee company targets small coffeehouses by saturating the market with closely spaced Starbucks stores, buying out competitors' leases, or paying premiums for real estate that small coffeehouses cannot afford. These practices all mark small businesses for failure and force them out. Consumers lose, because there is less competition; less choice results in higher prices. The company has been dubbed anticompetitive by some. Starbucks definitely does have a strategy to achieve and maintain a dominant market position, but this is a highly debated issue in coffee circles, so let's examine both sides of the debate on this issue, and you can be the judge.

The anticompetitive debate has been fueled in recent years by a 2006 antitrust lawsuit filed by Penny Stafford, who is a Bellevue, Washington, coffee shop owner. Stafford contended that Starbucks illegally blocked her from opening competing stores. As the *Seattle Weekly* reported on September 26, 2006, "Penny Stafford, who owns Belvi Coffee and Tea Exchange, says she was locked out of the best office space in Bellevue and Seattle by Starbucks' exclusive leasing agreements with landlords. She finally rented space to sell espresso inside a deli, but says her customers were inundated with free samples from Starbucks employees who worked nearby." On April 29, 2008, the federal case was closed. Mediation resulted in an undisclosed settlement.

Earlier, critics claimed that Starbucks bought out the competition. Indeed, the quickest way to grow is through mergers and acquisitions. In 1998, the Starbucks Corporation acquired the Seattle Coffee Company of Britain in a stock swap worth around $83 million. The British retailer had 60-plus stores, and they were all rebranded with the Starbucks name. The action quickly made Starbucks the leading specialty coffee company in Britain, but it did not come without naysayers.

A British Broadcasting Corporation News story painted a harsh picture of the coffee invasion:

> As the competition struggled to compete, Starbucks kept running its expensive sites at a loss, prompting accusations that they were using their muscle to unfairly squeeze out the opposition.
>
> Starbucks didn't just upset its rivals. Its drive for world dominance meant it was becoming a symbol of globalization, and therefore a target for protestors (BBC News, *Store Wars: Cappuccino Kings*, June 9, 2004).

Starbucks did it again in 2003, by purchasing the U.S.–based Seattle Coffee Company, which included Seattle's Best Coffee and Torrefazione Italia. The cost? A cool $72 million in cash. That is a huge amount of money—$72 followed by six zeros, or $72,000,000. Only the big boys and girls, like Starbucks, have access to that kind of money. A mom-and-pop business may only have $72 in the cash register, without the million-dollar pockets of the global giant.

What did Starbucks get in the deal? Starbucks got 129 Seattle's Best Coffee cafes and 21 Torrefazione Italia cafes. In 2005, Starbucks announced that all Torrefazione Italia cafés, which replicated the Italian coffee bar experience, would be closed by year's end. Although all the stores are gone now, the coffee brand is alive through online purchase, in select grocery stores, and in food-service establishments. Today, Seattle's Best Coffee has more than 540 cafes in the United States, as well as 86 espresso bars; plus, the brand's coffee products are available nationwide in supermarkets and at more than 3,900 food-service locations.

There is often a fine line between true competition and anticompetitive moves. The United States, along with most other countries, has laws to thwart anticompetitive strategies. If there are any serious issues, it is up to the government—not public opinion—to restrain activity. Despite a governmental Department of Justice watchdog, Starbucks has lost the favor of some consumers on a moral basis, because of its strategy to maintain a dominant position in the business world.

Case in point: In 1999, roughly 50,000 people gathered in Seattle to protest the World Trade Organization (WTO)'s third Ministerial Conference, which took place from November 29 to December 4. The WTO is an international voluntary-membership organization that sets the rules for global trade. It promotes economic globalization and free trade, which some view as in favor of big multinational corporations. So the street protests were a result of an antiglobalization movement, and protestors were angry about some of the methods Starbucks has used to expand its market share. Properties in downtown Seattle owned by multinationals were deliberately vandalized. The Seattle-based Starbucks was one of many targets, and several Starbucks stores were vandalized by anticorporate rioters.

The other side of the coin is that some local mom-and-pop stores are actually helped by Starbucks. Starbucks has deep pockets and does a tremendous amount of advertising. The mom-and-pop stores don't always have money in their budgets for ads, but Starbucks has increased knowledge about and awareness of coffee and specialty blends for everybody in the $12 billion-plus specialty coffee industry. Small coffee shops may see some positive spin-off effects from Starbucks' very presence. According to a recent publication from the Specialty Coffee Association of America, the majority—57 percent—of the nation's coffeehouses are still independents with 1 to 3 units, aka mom-and-pop stores. Only 40 percent are chains (10-plus units), while 3 percent are micro-chains (4 to 9 units). Starbucks just might have increased business for everyone, big and small alike. Years ago, a cup of coffee was just a way to wake up in the morning or stay alert at night; Starbucks made drinking coffee the in-thing to do.

Coffee Talk

According to the Specialty Coffee Association of America, it takes about 42 coffee beans to make an average serving of espresso.

UNION STRUGGLES

Starbucks employees—or partners, as they are called—have always been an important part of the company. The coffee giant touts itself as the socially responsible company. Starbucks has always made it a point to provide great benefits to partners—health insurance for full- and part-time employees; Bean Stock that permits partial ownership of the company; and a 1-pound bag of free coffee each week. Sounds like a fabulous deal, right? Well, apparently not to everyone who works for the coffee giant. In 2004, the first Starbucks employee union was formed.

The Starbucks Workers Union (SWU) was formed to organize the retail employees of Starbucks. Some of the more vocal complaints from partners involve bad hours, low pay, and insurance they can't afford. The SWU members are interested in strong wage strength, working hours, and job climate. SWU is a part of the Industrial Workers of the World (IWW) union. The IWW has a long history that dates back to the early 1900s. So far, the SWU has had some success at recruitment, mainly in the states of New York, Michigan, and Illinois. Starbucks workers belong to a select group of unions in Canada, Australia, and New Zealand, too. But, overall, the numbers appear modest—just 300 members, according to a December 30, 2008, *Business Week* article.

On December 23, 2008, the National Labor Relations Board (NLRB), an independent federal agency created by Congress to administer the National Labor Relations Act, ruled that Starbucks had engaged in unfair labor practices. There have been other NLRB issues in recent years, but this ruling has been the strongest to date. The ruling stems from the company's efforts to counter the IWW Starbucks Workers Union. The IWW filed charges against Starbucks, claiming, among other things, that three New York baristas were fired for supporting the union.

Starbucks has appealed the charge. The ruling, 88 pages in total length, was prepared by Administrative Law Judge Mindy E. Landow and states that the company interrogated employees, implemented new policies, more strictly enforced old policies, and, finally, disciplined and discharged employees in retaliation for their support of the union at several of its retail coffee stores in New York. Judge Landow ordered that the three former baristas be reinstated and compensated for loss of earnings. Starbucks was ordered to end discriminatory treatment of other pro-union workers. Additional highlights include that the company cannot prohibit employees from discussing the union while they are off duty; cannot punish employees with poor evaluations because they support the union; and must not fire employees because they support the union. Starbucks settled another case in 2006, in which it agreed to stop antiunion actions.

The SWU has a Web site at www.starbucksunion.org, where it specifically states its purpose. "The Starbucks Workers Union is an organization of employees at the world's largest coffee chain united for a living wage, secure work hours, and respect on the job. We are part of the Industrial Workers of the World, a union for all workers. Working together, we have won improvements in wages and working conditions and remedied individual grievances with management."

In his 1997 book about Starbucks, founder and CEO Schultz writes about the care with which he believes employees should be treated. Clearly, he believes he treats his employees well. "If there's one accomplishment I'm proudest of at Starbucks, it's the relationship of trust and confidence we've built with the people who work at the company. That's not just an empty phrase, as it is with so many companies," Schultz wrote (Schultz and Yang 1997, 6). "We treat warehouse workers and entry-level retail people with the kind of respect that most companies show for only high executives."

In fact, in an August 8, 2006, press release fact sheet, Starbucks strongly states its position on union representation of partners. "Starbucks firmly believes that the direct employment relationship which we currently have with our partners is the best way to help ensure a great work environment. We believe we do not need a third party to act on behalf of our partners. We prefer to deal directly with them in a fair and respectful manner, just as we have throughout our history."

The SWU is not the only union that has had issues with the company. The International Union of Operating Engineers Local 286 had an encounter with Starbucks a few years ago. It used to represent Starbucks maintenance mechanics and technicians at the company's Kent, Washington, roasting plant. The union no longer represents the workers, but in 2005, Starbucks settled charges the union had filed with the NLRB, accusing the company of systematically screening out job applicants who had previously worked at unionized employers or had other perceived union sympathies. In 2005, Starbucks paid out $165,000 to eight employees of this facility to settle charges that they had been retaliated against for being pro-union. Starbucks was accused of screening out individuals who had any pro-union connections. The charge also said the company dismissed an employee because he would not continue this practice. The company did not admit to any wrongdoing. However, it did agree to pay the employee $125,000 and to pay $5,000 and offer employment to each of eight individuals who had earlier been turned down for jobs.

Starbucks reports an employee count of 176,000 workers worldwide and clearly has a long record of employee support and social responsibility. For a company that claims to value its partners, a hint at unfair labor practices is definitely disappointing and most definitely unwanted press. These are issues of which the company is no doubt mindful.

Coffee Talk

Take a 10-minute break and test your brain. Give yourself two minutes for each term and see if you can find all the words hidden in these coffee- and tea-related words. Keep it simple—no proper names, please.

BAG BEAN BREW COFFEE TEA

Answers: BAG (a, ab, gab); BEAN (a, ab, an, ban, bane, be, nab, neb [a beak or bill]); BREW (be, re [the second note of a major scale], we, web); COFFEE (fee, foe, of, off); TEA (a, ate, eat).

ETHOSWATER CONTROVERSY

EthosWater is a bottled-water company with a social mission: "helping children around the world get clean water and raising awareness of the World Water Crisis." (www.ethoswater.com) The Ethos brand emerged from an idea Peter Thum developed after working on a consulting project in South Africa. The former strategy consultant noticed that many people there did not have access to clean drinking water. After researching this problem around the world and consulting on a project in the bottled-water industry, he realized there was an opportunity to create a new bottled-water brand that could help children and their communities have access to safe water through its sales. In 2002, Thum left his job to envision and develop EthosWater; he brought in friend and business school roommate Jonathan Greenblatt a year later to be his partner.

Thum and Greenblatt founded EthosWater in 2003. What is unique about their company is that a percentage of its profits go to support clean-water programs in developing countries, including India, Ethiopia, Honduras, and Kenya. For every bottle of water that Ethos sells, 5 cents are donated toward solving the world water crisis.

On the back of each clear plastic bottle, with the words scattered across a map of the world, the impressive details are explained for the consumer:

OUR MISSION

We began with a simple idea: "Let's create a bottled water to help children around the world get clean water." We felt compelled to make a difference, because more than 1 billion people lack clean water access, and the problem affects children most. EthosWater donates 5 cents for every bottle sold toward humanitarian water programs. Our current goal is to invest $10 million in these programs by 2010. Already, we're helping children and their communities in Africa, Asia and Latin America. Thank you for joining us in our efforts.

Peter Thum and Jonathan Greenblatt, Founders

Doesn't the mission sound wonderful? It gets better. As of early 2009, Ethos clean-water grant commitments already exceed $6.2 million. Each upscale bottle—attractive and relatively expensive (I paid $1.80 for the 23.7-ounce bottle at Starbucks)—raises awareness of the world water crisis for those who read the print embossed on the plastic. It should make customers feel very good—not only do they quench their thirst when they buy this water, but they help fund clean-water projects in struggling countries around the world.

Thum and Greenblatt self-funded the launch of Ethos and even made the first deliveries out of an old Volvo station wagon. But now, the vision has been taken to a whole new level. EthosWater was acquired by Starbucks in 2005 for $7.7 million, giving the bottled-water company a much larger distribution channel. Thum became vice president of Starbucks and sits on the board of directors of the Starbucks Foundation. He manages Ethos' business strategy and directs its philanthropic work. Greenblatt served for a time as vice president of global consumer products at Starbucks and also served on the Starbucks Foundation. He left the company in 2006 to spend time with his family.

This sounds like such a worthy cause; it is hard to believe it has generated controversy. According to the product's Web site, www.ethoswater. com, the name Ethos is even derived from the Greek *ethos,* meaning the distinguishing character, sentiment, moral nature, or guiding beliefs of a person, group or institution. The slang reference to the water calls it ethics in a bottle. But there has been a tremendous amount of hullabaloo about the clean-water company. Let us investigate the issues.

EthosWater is sold at most Starbucks locations throughout North America. The water is also available at premium retail stores, major grocery stores, and convenience and drug stores. Each bottle states that 5 cents from its sale will be donated to fund humanitarian water programs. Proponents may say this is one quick and easy way for the typical consumer to practice social responsibility. And, of course, for those junior economists out there, don't forget that EthosWater creates jobs. Employment is good for the economy and gets money circulating through the system. But the controversy is multifold. Some people think that by selling EthosWater, Starbucks is cashing in on a humanitarian effort. Ethos is a for-profit branch of Starbucks, and only a small portion of each sale goes to charity. Even though 2008 was a down year for Starbucks, the company had net earnings of nearly $700 million two years earlier, in 2006. By 2010, Ethos wants to raise $10 million for humanitarian water programs; this is just a fraction of Starbucks' revenue in a good year.

Critics claim EthosWater is a way for the company to make money and more should be donated to aid. The 5 cents-per-bottle is not significant enough. Others argue that buying water is not a good use of consumer funds—instead, they say, fill up a thermos with tap water and donate the entire $1.80 you would pay for the bottled water. And there is one more point of contention: On the bottles is printed "PLEASE RECYCLE," but everyone knows that not all the bottles will be recycled; some will go to landfills.

The National Resources Defense Council is a nonprofit organization with a mission to safeguard the Earth, its people, its plants and animals, and the natural systems on which all life depends. According to this organization, "Most bottled water comes in recyclable PET plastic bottles, but only about 13 percent of the bottles we use get recycled. In 2005, 2 million tons of plastic water bottles ended up clogging landfills instead of getting recycled." So a company with a social mission to help bring clean water to many people may be adding to the plastic pollution problem of others. There are undoubtedly some Ethos bottles lying around in landfills. It might be better to enjoy your tap water and reduce the plastic in our environment. It seems counterintuitive to help children in other countries but create more waste and pollution here at home.

It's definitely a social dilemma. What do you think? Is this is wonderful business idea that raises money for the sorely needed water projects in underdeveloped countries? Or is it simply another way for Starbucks to make a profit?

CONCERNS ABOUT PAPER CUPS

Apart from the Ethos plastic water bottle controversy, Starbucks largely gets high marks for its environmentally friendly focus. The U.S. Environmental Protection Agency (EPA) ranked Starbucks number 17 on its Top 50 Green Power Partners list in October 2008 for its purchases of renewable energy. The company even has a green guru, Ben Packard, Starbucks' vice president of corporate social responsibility, who leads the coffee company in its efforts to minimize environmental impact.

The coffee company's environmental goals are lofty. By 2010, Starbucks has a goal of reducing energy use by 25 percent in all company-operated and international stores. But what about the cups? The one area Starbucks fans and foes alike seem to concentrate on is that Starbucks' paper cups are not recyclable. Okay, that sure doesn't sound like the environmental leader applauded above, but there is more to the story.

Starbucks cups can't be recycled because they contain both paper and plastic. It is actually the plastic lining that makes them nonrecyclable. Starbucks uses a plastic cup lining so hot beverages will not seep through into the paper layer. The kick is that most recycling centers can only recycle products made of 100 percent paper or 100 percent plastic, not a hybrid of the two.

The company explained its actions in a statement issued September 18, 2007:

> Starbucks' white paper cups, used for hot beverages, are made of paper fiber and the industry standard liner (low-density polyethylene plastic). The paper provides the rigidity for the cup, while the plastic layer keeps the paper layer intact by protecting it from the hot beverage. This plastic layer also makes the hot beverage cups unrecyclable in most paper recycling systems. We are continually evaluating alternatives to the current plastic coating, and are currently conducting life cycle assessments for bio-based plastics.

Starbucks uses a lot of cups; it bought 2.5 billion paper cups in 2007. What a powerful impact it would be if this amount of trash could be recycled. The company does tout that the cups are made with 10 percent post-consumer recycled fiber (PCF), and in 2006, it was the very first company in the United States to use this percentage of PCF in its hot beverage cups. The beverage sleeves are made of corrugated 60 percent PCF.

The print on each corrugated jacket couldn't make Starbucks' environmental stance any clearer, stating "Starbucks is committed to reducing our environmental impact through increased use of post-consumer recycled materials. Help us help the planet." According to the Environmental Defense Paper Calculator (www.papercalculator.org), using 10 percent PCF in 2.5 billion cups means 11,300 fewer tons of wood are consumed, the equivalent of 78,000 trees a year. The PCF cups may be a little more expensive, but Starbucks thinks they are worth it, because they provide a more environmentally friendly option.

If the lack of recyclable cups bothers you, you can help in the pursuit of a greener world in other ways. Starbucks gives a 10-cent discount when customers bring their own reusable cups. And if you stay in the store to drink your coffee, be sure to ask for one of the ceramic "for here" mugs provided by the coffeehouse. Starbucks says customers in the United States and Canada took advantage of the 10-cent discount offer nearly 20 million times in fiscal 2007 by bringing their own reusable cups into stores. This opportunity kept roughly 758,000 pounds of paper from winding up in a landfill.

Recycling Coffee Grounds

While we are looking at the subject of recycling, here's something else for you to consider. Though Starbucks' coffee cups are not recyclable, its coffee grounds *are* recyclable. Where, you ask? The answer may surprise you—in your garden. While it started as a grassroots initiative by a team of store partners, Starbucks began its Grounds for Your Garden program on a national basis in 2000. And, better yet, it is free of charge. Used coffee grounds for compost are available at any retail location across North America, based on availability.

Composting at home begins with kitchen scraps, fruit and vegetable peels, leaves and grass clippings, and, yes, coffee grounds. Check out Starbucks' Web site at www.starbucks.com/aboutus/compost.asp for further details on how to get your garden off to a great start. Here are a few general tips included on the site:

- Coffee grounds act as a green material with a carbon-nitrogen (C-N) ratio of 20 to 1. Combined with brown materials, such as leaves and straw, coffee grounds generate heat and will speed up the composting process.

- Coffee grounds can be applied directly as a top dressing to acid-loving plants, such as blueberries, hydrangeas, and azaleas. (Acid-loving plants thrive in areas where rainfall is common in the warm season.) Adding brown material, such as leaves and dried grass clippings, to the mulch will help keep a balanced soil pH.
- And here's one I bet you did not know: Coffee grounds are wonderful for your worm bin, too. Red worms fed with coffee grounds and other vegetarian materials will flourish, turning scraps into garden-nourishing compost.

Note only does Starbucks provide spent coffee grounds to its customers, but the company also recycles and donates grounds for compost to organizations such as parks, schools, and nurseries in order to reduce waste. Starbucks makes a hugely positive environmental footprint with its program to recycle its grounds.

Author's note: After researching this great opportunity, I drove to my local Starbucks for a sample bag of spent coffee grounds. After my request for compost material, I was cheerfully and politely told, "We don't have any grounds made up, but we will happily put some together if you can wait just a moment. Within seconds, I was carrying out a huge Starbucks shopping bag of used coffee grounds. I am sold on the opportunity and have been happily composting ever since. My suggestion? Follow Starbucks' lead and turn organic waste into a medium that will grow absolutely beautiful gardens.

Coffee Quiz

WHEN DID COFFEE BECOME A SUBSTITUTE
FOR TEA IN AMERICA?

   a. When American colonists became angry over a tea tax
   b. When farmers started to grow coffee in the Midwest
   c. When coffee bushes flourished widely in parks and forests
   d. When all tea bushes stopped producing tea leaves.

If you guessed "a. When American colonists became angry over a tea tax," you are correct. That means either you are a good guesser or you remember some details about the Boston Tea Party from history class. Either way, here's a quick history lesson review.

Coffee was introduced in North America circa 1668, but it didn't become popular as an American drink until after the famous Boston Tea Party of 1773. On December 16, 1773, a group of colonists, disguised as American Indians, boarded three British ships and dumped 342 crates of tea into Boston Harbor. That was a lot of tea—45 tons of it. It was a direct act of protest by American colonists who were angry at the British government. Three years before, in 1770, colonial opposition and boycotting of imported British goods had caused the British Parliament to withdraw all of the Townshend Act's taxes, except one; it retained the heavy tax on imported British tea.

The situation remained relatively quiet as American colonists simply evaded the tax by smuggling tea into the colonies from Holland. But this was not good for the British East India Company, which had been left with huge surpluses of tea and was financially faltering. The British government wanted to save the tea company from bankruptcy. So, in May 1773, Parliament gave the company a refund, or *drawback,* of the entire shilling-per-pound duty, which allowed the company to sell tea more cheaply than the Dutch smugglers. It was assumed that Americans would buy the cheaper tea, despite the tax, rather than the higher-priced smuggled tea from Holland. This would uphold the principle of parliamentary taxation and also save the tea company from ruin. American colonists condemned the act. They saw it as taxation without representation, and many people boycotted buying and drinking tea as a protest. Although the movement away from tea was short-lived, coffee became a fashionable drink and a substitute for tea.

STARBUCKS COPES WITH TRAGEDY

Starbucks has had its share of sadness through the years. Notably, late on July 6, 1997, after a long Fourth of July weekend, tragedy struck at a Georgetown Starbucks Coffee shop in Washington, D.C. Early on that Monday morning, at 5:15 A.M., the dayshift manager arrived to find three Starbucks employees shot to death in an apparent botched theft. Nothing had been stolen, and no fingerprints were left at the scene. A bullet hole was found over the safe, but the safe had not been opened. Starbucks offered a $100,000 reward for information leading to the arrest and conviction of the person or people responsible for the crime, and $10,000 was put up by the Georgetown Business Association. Forensic psychologist and Tru TV's Crime Library contributor Katherine Ramsland wrote about the case on www.trutv.com:

... Starbucks decided to reopen the shop, announcing a reopening date of February 21, 1998. To honor the victims, they built a floor-to-ceiling Maplewood mural that held three boxes, each engraved with the initials of one of the victims. Their surviving relatives placed mementos into the boxes, and the company announced it would donate all net profits from this store to the Community Foundation for the National Capital Region, an organization dedicated to nonviolence. Starbucks also gave money to

Circle of Hope, a group that guided teens toward being produc-
tive members of society.

In June 1998, after an *America's Most Wanted* segment on the shootings had
aired on TV for a second time, a tip came in that pointed to Carl Derek
Cooper. Cooper, a DC-area man in his late 20s, was arrested and brought
to justice. Finally, on April 25, 2000, he avoided a possible death sentence
by pleading guilty to a multitude of crimes, including the three Starbucks
employee murders. The judge sentenced him to life in prison with no
chance of parole.

More recently, tragedy struck again at a Starbucks store in St. Louis,
Missouri. A Good Samaritan, 54-year-old Roger Kreutz, was struck by a car
while trying to prevent a crime. He died from his injuries two days later.
Kreutz was a regular at his local Starbucks coffee shop and witnessed two
thieves stealing the tip jar money. He ran outside Starbucks chasing them
and was run over by the getaway car. The thieves left the scene but were
later apprehended. There was only around $5 in the tip jar.

Coffee Talk

According to the Specialty Coffee Association of America, Americans
drink more than 300 million cups of coffee each day. About 75 percent
of those cups are home-brewed.

COMPETITION PERCOLATES

As consumers refine their taste for specialty coffee, more businesses
have jumped into the gourmet market (see Table 7.1). Add a down economy
to the increasing number of retail coffee sellers and it is an all-out war to see
who will make the most coffee cash. Starbucks may be the cream of the crop
among retail coffeehouses, but it definitely has to keep its eyes open to its
longtime competition at Caribou Coffee Company and Peet's Coffee & Tea.

Caribou Coffee Company

Caribou Coffee Company is the second-largest company-owned
gourmet coffeehouse operator in the United States, behind Starbucks.
The company was founded in 1992 and has its headquarters in Min-
neapolis, Minnesota. Its distinctive stores are designed to resemble ski
lodges. There are over 500 Caribou locations in 19 states and the District
of Columbia, as well as in two overseas markets. Over 6,000 individuals
are employed by the company, whose mission is to provide a total experience that makes the day better. While Caribou is dwarfed by Starbucks'
more than 16,000 stores and roughly 176,000 employees, it provides some
serious competition. In 2005, the company went public and now trades

Table 7.1
Comparing the Competition

	Starbucks	McDonald's	Dunkin' Donuts	Peet's	Caribou
Sales	$10.4 billion	$23.5 billion	$5.5 billion	$284.8 million	$253.9 million
Net Income	$315.5 million	$4.3 billion	Privately held	$11.2 million	($16.3 million) (net loss)
Net Profit Margin	3.0 percent	18.34 percent	Privately held	3.92 percent	-6.4 percent
Approximate Number of Stores	16,680	31,377	8,835	166	511

on the NASDAQ. Caribou Coffee focuses on providing extraordinary coffee to its customers through several avenues, including grocery stores, its online store, and its coffeehouses, which feature a warm, relaxing, and welcoming environment.

Caribou Coffee sells high-quality gourmet coffee beverages and specialty drinks, whole-bean coffee, specialty teas, baked goods, and brewing supplies. The company sells its products to grocers, mass retailers, office coffee providers, airlines, hotels, sports and entertainment venues, college campuses, and others. It is also involved with some third-party licensing, allowing use of the Caribou brand on food and merchandise. The company is struggling with reduced U.S. store traffic, just as Starbucks is, and is committed to cutting costs and improving profitability. There is no evidence that profitability is improving yet. For fiscal 2008, reports show that revenue fell to $253.9 million from $256.8 million the year before. The company reported a loss of $16.3 million, though this was down from a loss of $30.7 million a year earlier. Caribou posted a profit of $1.3 million in the fourth quarter of 2008, however, so Starbucks should note the positive trend.

Caribou may be number two, but the much smaller company doesn't have a problem taking on Starbucks. The week Starbucks announced it would regularly brew decaf coffee in its stores only until noon, in an effort to save costs, with decaf brewed after noon on request, Caribou reacted: It announced it would be giving away 12-ounce cups of decaf coffee starting at noon Friday, January 30, 2009. All Caribou Coffee locations offered free decaffeinated coffee from noon until closing that day. According to a Caribou Coffee press release dated January 29, 2009, "Decaf drinkers deserve better," said Alfredo Martel, Caribou Coffee senior vice president of marketing. "Caribou Coffee is first and foremost a coffeehouse, emphasis on coffee. We strive to give our customers the very best coffee, when, where, and how they want it. And if that means a cup of decaffeinated coffee in the afternoon, then we're more than happy to oblige. We invite all decaf coffee drinkers to experience Caribou Coffee's exceptional customer service by tasting a truly delicious cup of our Natural Decaf coffee on the house."

Peet's Coffee & Tea

Are you familiar with the saying "slow and steady wins the race"? If this slogan could be applied to any of the major specialty coffee retailers, it would be Peet's Coffee & Tea, Inc. Peet's is a specialty coffee roaster and marketer of high-quality whole-bean arabica coffee. The company also offers tea, specialty drinks, baked goods, and coffee and tea merchandise. The company was founded in 1966, when Dutch roaster Alfred Peet opened his first retail coffee shop in Berkeley, California. Remember—it was Peet who taught the original three Starbucks founders how to roast coffee, and it was Peet's company that supplied Starbucks with its quality roasted beans for its first year of business.

The old-time coffee company has built its reputation on hand-roasting small batches of superior quality beans, as well as on the freshness of those beans. It is largely a financially conservative company and has followed a steady pattern of growth. Over the past four decades, Peet's has secured a loyal following by attracting those who appreciate quality coffee—Peetnicks, as they are called. The original Peetnicks were faithful customers of the original Berkeley store. Today, consumers who appreciate the very best in coffee and tea can join the Peetnicks community through the company's Web site and receive a discount when ordering products online. The company currently has 166 retail stores in California, Colorado, Illinois, Massachusetts, Oregon, and Washington State. In addition to its company-owned and -operated stores, Peet's sells its coffee through over 250 grocery stores; via home delivery, office, and restaurant accounts; to food-service companies; and online through its Web site.

The company, based in Emeryville, California, went public in 2001 and trades on the NASDAQ under the symbol PEET. Peet's has a market capitalization—a measure of the company's value—of $284 million. That is small compared to the mega coffee company Starbucks, which has a market capitalization of roughly $7 billion, but Peet's is a powerful force. This little dynamo is serious competition. Historically, its balance sheet, income statement, and profitability ratios have been healthy. Peet's believes investment in business pays off. For fiscal year 2008, Peet's reported that net revenue grew 14 percent to $284.8 million, compared with $249.4 million in 2007. It also said its net income rose from $8.4 million in 2007 to $11.2 million for 2008. Net profit for the 2008 fiscal year stood at a respectable 3.9 percent, up from 3.4 the prior year. And profits look respectable, growing to $4 million, or 29 cents per share, compared with $3.3 million, or 23 cents per share, for the same quarter the year before.

In a Peet's Coffee & Tea press release dated February 12, 2009, Patrick O'Dea, president and CEO, said, "We are pleased with our results for the quarter and full year." He continued, "Real productivity improvements resulting from past investments we've made are improving margins as we move forward." The company's investments in the business certainly did prove wise, as the numbers make clear. Along with achieving its earnings forecast for 2008, Peet's expects substantial improvement in earnings performance again in 2009, despite the downturn in the economy.

Looking beyond the big three, the coffee war is definitely heating up behind the old-timer's venue. Local mom-and-pop stores with lots of seating, a friendly atmosphere, and generally lower prices are serious competitors for the coffee dollar. And among chain names, everywhere you look, Starbucks has competition—Wendy's, Burger King, Panera Bread, and many more are in the coffee game. Among others, there are two new heavy hitters to the java market: Dunkin' Donuts and McDonald's are playing hardball. Although the gloves have definitely come off, Starbucks seems to be taking it all in stride.

Dunkin' Donuts

When it was founded in 1950, Dunkin' Donuts coffee was simply second to the baked goods it was known for. Hey—it has 52 varieties of donuts! But the privately held company, based in Canton, Massachusetts, has recently begun a hard push for its coffee line. Dunkin' Donuts sells nearly 1.5 billion cups of coffee each year. Today, it offers ground and whole-bean coffee in a range of flavored blends, also with espresso drinks, iced coffee, latte drinks, hot chocolate, smoothies, and more, with beverage sales making up 63 percent of domestic sales. You can even find Dunkin' Donuts coffee at the grocery store.

Like Starbucks, this company offers customers rechargeable Dunkin' Donuts Cards as part of marketing its products—a fast and convenient way to pay for items at the Dunkin' Donuts shops that participate in the program. It also has an online store that offers coffee, tea, and Dunkin' Donuts merchandise, including T-shirts, hats, and blankets, as well as brewing equipment. Dunkin' Donuts is a subsidiary of Dunkin' Brands, Inc., which holds another highly recognized brand name: Baskin-Robbins, a favored neighborhood ice cream shop. At the end of 2008, there were 8,835 Dunkin' Donuts stores worldwide in a total of 31 countries. Global sales for the Dunkin' Donuts company were $5.5 billion.

An aggressive campaign aimed at Starbucks makes the competition even steeper. A Dunkin' Donuts press release dated October 20, 2008, touts a national television spot depicting "hard-working Americans who take a blind taste test during their busy daily routines." The spot suggests that participants preferred Dunkin' Donuts coffee over Starbucks in the taste test. The company calls attention to the ads on radio, in shops, and online. Dunkin' Donuts has even created a Web site for the ad campaign, www. dunkinbeatstarbucks.com. You can get more details on the independent taste test, which was conducted by AIG Research Inc., on that site.

A new, $100 million ad campaign began in January 2009 with the theme "You Kin' Do It." But it is just one more example of the aggressive campaign that continues for the coffee drinker's dollars and just another day at the shop for the giant Starbucks. It proves that coffee is indeed a tough business, but Starbucks has made it clear—it is in the game and here to stay.

McDonald's

Fast-food giant McDonald's, based in Oak Brook, Illinois, has been around since 1948. As of December 31, 2007, McDonald's Corporation operated 31,377 restaurants in 118 countries. It is one of the elite 30 stocks in the Dow Jones Industrial Average, a blue-chip stock that is an industry leader. Revenue is huge, at $23.5 billion for fiscal 2008, compared with $22.8 billion the previous year. The profit margin jumped up to 18.2 percent for fiscal 2008, from 10.2 percent the previous year.

Mickey D's, as the company is sometimes informally called, is known for convenience and a value-priced menu. Early in 2008, the company announced a national rollout of made-to-order specialty coffee brews— mochas, lattes, cappuccinos. By late 2008, McDonald's had added the McCafe coffee drinks to more than 3,000 of its nearly 14,000 U.S. locations. The next step is to work on broadening consumers' thinking beyond burgers and fries when they think of McDonald's. You've probably seen new ads for the drinks on TV. There's even a special McCafe Web site to promote the premium line of coffees, www.wakeuptowhatsnew.com, where you can learn about the drinks and do a little cappuccino art. There is also UnsnobbyCoffee.com, where you can host a snobby coffee intervention, play pinball, locate McCafe locations, or get educated about the coffee line. It was designed to promote the company's launch of its premium drinks in a fun-centered way. McDonald's is using old-fashioned billboard advertising, too. The *Seattle Post-Intelligencer* reported on December 10, 2008, that McDonald's had erected a billboard in plain sight of Starbucks' headquarters in Seattle, with the signage "Four bucks is dumb. Now serving espresso." Who do you think that was targeting?

YOU DECIDE

True Competition?

Should Dunkin' Donuts and McDonald's, both with more moderately priced coffee options, really be considered true competition for Starbucks? I took an informal survey to find out. I sampled prices in three Midwest cities and noted the prices paid for similarly sized (10-ounce and 12-ounce) cups of brewed coffee. The figures below show the average price charged by each retailer, before any tax.

McDonald's small (12 ounces)	**$0.99**
Dunkin' Donuts small (10 ounces)	**$1.26**
Starbucks tall (12 ounces)	**$1:65**

Try doing a cost comparison at your local stores to get a feel for the price variations. Likely, you will find a somewhat similar trend.

McDonald's	_____
Dunkin' Donuts	_____
Starbucks	_____

Think about the customer base and atmosphere, too. Starbucks offers a high-quality, upper-end coffee drink in a relaxed, comfortable atmosphere. You have likely visited a Dunkin' Donuts or a McDonald's store, perhaps hundreds of time in your life. Do you think McDonald's and Dunkin' Donuts customers are potential customers for the premium coffee shop Starbucks? Dunkin' Donuts and McDonald's are both known for quick counter service or get-it-to-go service at the drive-thru window. Meanwhile, Starbucks coffee drinkers may be more likely to sit down, enjoy the surroundings, read a newspaper, or work on their laptops while sipping a premium espresso. Think about it.

Let's say you are a customer relations expert for Carole's Coffee Consulting. You have been asked to answer one simple question for an upcoming marketing meeting: "Describe in three words each what the customers at Dunkin' Donuts, McDonald's, and Starbucks want most from their coffee purchase." It is just a fun little exercise, but it makes you think.

Dunkin' Donut customers want _____, _____, and _____.

McDonald's customers want _____, _____, and _____.

Starbucks customers want _____, _____, and _____.

If you used words like *fast service* and *convenience* for Dunkin' Donuts and McDonald's, you are not alone. Maybe the word *donuts* cropped up for Dunkin' Donuts or *hamburgers and fries* came up for McDonald's. You might have used words like *quality, comfort, premium, relaxing,* and so on for Starbucks. Maybe you had some new terms for Carole's Coffee Consulting's marketing meeting, too. Good for you. Does Starbucks have an edge on the premium coffee market? Exercises like these help determine who Starbucks' true competitors are—and sharpen your business acumen.

Chapter Eight

Transition and Future Prospects

Success should not be measured in dollars: It's about how you conduct the journey, and how big your heart is at the end of it.
— Howard Schultz, chairman and CEO of Starbucks,
Pour Your Heart into It (1997)

COMPANY FACES SLIDING STOCK PRICE

Starbucks Corporation went public on June 26, 1992, at a price of $17 per share (this equates to $0.53 per share, adjusted for five subsequent stock splits). It closed on the first day of trading at $21.50 (or $0.67 per share, on a split-adjusted basis). The stock is traded on the National Association of Securities Dealers Automated Quotations (NASDAQ), the largest U.S. electronic stock market, under the symbol SBUX. Starbucks hit its high in 2006 at $40 per share and has traded mostly downhill since. Nevertheless, the shares show a positive uptick from their starting price.

As of 2009, the Coffee King faces lower demand from a recessionary economy. Sales are down, and the stock price is falling. Watch it for relative highs and lows, particularly against others in the industry. Check out the trends on McDonald's (MCD), Peet's Coffee & Tea (PEET), and Caribou Coffee (CBOU). (Dunkin' Donuts is privately held, meaning it has no stock price to track.) All of these retail establishments have taken a tumble over the past year (see Table 8.1).

Although Starbucks shares spiraled downward in 2008, in early 2009, the company's stock price was fluctuating in the $10 range, holding its own in the depressed economy. The company's high during the prior year was $18.99, versus a low of $7.06. The volume of trading in Starbucks was high at 13,789,910, roughly the same amount of share activity as for the mega fast-food giant Mickey D's. All others have lost value off their highs from earlier checkbook balances. Starbucks' stock lost roughly half its value in 2008, but all stocks are selling lower during the economic glut.

8888888888888888

Table 8.1
Stock Market Comparisons

February 27, 2009	Starbucks (SBUX)	McDonald's (MCD)	Dunkin' Donuts (N/A)	Peet's (PEET)	Caribou (CBOU)
Closing Stock Price	$9.15	$52.45	Privately held—N/A	$21.55	$1.67
52-Week High	$18.99	$67	N/A	$29.75	$3.48
52-Week Low	$7.06	$45.75	N/A	$17.79	$1.10
Volume	13,789,910	13,384,800	N/A	150,573	6,599

Starbucks Scramble

Let's interrupt all these numbers and have some fun. Take a few moments to unscramble these mixed-up words. You get a clue for each one, but it's your job to test your brain and untangle the letters.

1.	PNERARST	Clue: Starbucks employees
2.	OSTHE	Clue: Five cents for every bottle sold goes to humanitarian water programs
3.	RAICAAB	Clue: Type of coffee bean purchased by Starbucks
4.	WADHOR	Clue: First name of Starbucks' CEO
5.	NOVANVI	Clue: Starbucks' smoothie-style drink

Answers: 1. partners; 2. Ethos; 3. arabica; 4. Howard; 5. Vivanno

---

HOW TO READ STARBUCKS' FINANCIAL SNAPSHOT

Snapshots and overviews of a stock are all similar in content and pack a powerful punch of information. Starbucks is listed on the Global Select (GS) Market, which means it meets the highest initial listing standards of any exchange in the world. Check out the trading symbol SBUX on any of the financial Internet sites, such as www.financeaol.com, www.finance google.com, www.financeyahoo.com, www.moneycentral.msn.com, www.money.cnn.com, or www.investingbusinessweek.com, and you can see up-to-date trading quote activity. You can also get such information as historical prices, stock charts, company news and information, headlines, and financials.

Here is an example of a snapshot quote after trading on Friday, January 2, 2009.

STARBUCKS CORPORATION. (SBUX: NASDAQ EXCHANGE)

LAST CLOSE 9.84 USD
+0.38 (+4.02%)
VOLUME 7.4 M

Open: $9.41	Previous Close: $9.46
High: $9.86	Low: $9.33
52 Wk High: $21.01	52 Wk Low: $7.06
Market Cap: 7.2B	Avg Vol: 3Mo 8.2M
Diluted EPS TTM: $0.43	Shares Out: 733.3M
Div: N/A	
Ex-Div. Date: N/A	Div. Yield: N/A
P/E TTM: 23.0X	

A great deal of information can be gleaned from just a quick overview. Starbucks Corporation is traded on the NASDAQ, with a trading symbol of SBUX. Starbucks also trades on other U.S. exchanges, such as the regional Cincinnati Stock Exchange (SBUX.C), and a multitude of foreign stock exchanges, such as the Berlin Stock Exchange (SBUX.BE), Frankfurt Stock Exchange (SBUX.F), and Mexico Stock Exchange (SBUX.MX). The code *USD* stands for U.S. dollars, to distinguish from other dollar-denominated currencies, such as the Canadian dollar. The stock closed on January 2 at $9.84; that was the last price of the day. If you wanted to buy a share of Starbucks stock, you would have had to pay $9.84 at that time. This was $0.38 higher than the previous close of $9.46 on December 31, 2008. (Remember that January 1 was New Year's Day and a stock market holiday.) Year-to-date performance was up 4.02 percent. Volume shows how many shares of SBUX were traded on a particular day, and in this case, there were 7.4 million shares of Starbucks stock traded on January 2, 2009. The trading volume information is good to take a look at, because a wide swing away from a typical trading day means there is some kind of news—either good or bad—that has caused investors to increase trading in Starbucks. This is pertinent information to know if you are an investor, and a good heads-up about some company-impacting news for Starbucks fans.

This stock opened the trading day at $9.41 per share and closed the previous day at $9.46. SBUX reached a high during the day of $9.86 (the best price if you were selling the stock), and a low of $9.33 (the deal of the day if you were buying the stock). Tip: You always want to buy low and sell high!

The 52-week range is the low and high of the price fluctuations of the stock over a one-year period. It was a turbulent year, with prices dipping down to $7.06 on November 21, 2008, after hitting a high of $21.01 on January 8, 2008. Keep in mind that we are looking at Starbucks during a recessionary period. In early 2006, by contrast, when economic times were better, SBUX stock even hit the $40 mark. So watch the stock price for relative highs and lows.

Market Cap stands for market capitalization and shows the total value of the company on a given day—here, roughly $7.2 billion. Investors look at the number as an indicator of company size. You get that figure by multiplying the stock price times the total number of shares outstanding. This number gives the total, theoretically, of what it would cost to buy the entire company. Here's a rough calculation: $9.84 × 733.3 million shares = $7.2 billion.

Volume shows that on average over the previous three months, there were 8.2 million shares traded daily. Again, this is good to know as a base on trading. A high number relative to the average volume says something in the economy is going on. It might be a major Gross Domestic Product (GDP) announcement, which is a benchmark output indicator for the entire U.S. economy; or it could be something happening within the company, such as a switch in the executive officers. That actually happened on Monday, January 7, 2008. It was announced that founder and Chairman Howard Schultz would immediately assume the role of CEO from Jim Donald, as Starbucks sales continued to weaken. Just to give you an idea of the impact of that news—on the Friday before the announcement (January 4), the stock closed with 20,052,900 shares traded. There were 25,240,400 shares traded the day of the announcement, and 63,148,800 shares were traded on January 8, the day following. That announcement generated a lot of buying and selling; plus, the company's shares rose 6.6 percent in after-hours trading following the announcement.

The earnings per share (EPS) figure is Starbucks' net income (over the trailing, or preceding, 12 months—TTM) divided by its number of shares outstanding. The simple EPS calculation uses just actual outstanding shares of a company's stock. Diluted EPS represents all potential stock that could be outstanding, with the impact of current stock-options grants and convertible bonds. It is a more stringent, conservative measure, like a worst-case situation. EPS can provide investors with an idea of a company's profitability and is one factor in how much investors would be willing to pay for the stock. Diluted EPS TTM is $0.43 on our example day, because it can represent the portion of the company's profit allocated to each potentially convertible (to common stock) share. Starbucks has 733.3 million shares outstanding, shares of Starbucks stock that are currently held by investors. This is good to know for figuring the potential value of the company, and such a high figure indicates that Starbucks is a widely held stock.

The P/E is the Price-to-Earnings Ratio. The P/E is calculated by taking the price of the stock and dividing it by the earnings per share of the stock. The earnings are usually taken from the TTM. The P/E tells, theoretically, how much an investor is willing to pay for $1 of a company's earnings. A P/E of 23 means that Starbucks has $1 in annual per-share earnings for every $23 in share price. P/E is often misinterpreted by the investment community and should really be viewed only in terms of long-term trends.

But, generally speaking, companies that are expected to grow and have higher earnings in the future should have a higher P/E than those that are in a downward trend. At a 23.0 P/E, the stock has a fairly high stock price compared to earnings, indicating that there may be high expectations for future earnings.

Dividends are the part of the net earnings of a company that are distributed to shareholders. Starbucks does not pay a dividend, so *Div.* and *Div. Yield* are not applicable to this stock. Also not applicable is *Ex-Div. Date,* which means without a dividend. If you buy a stock that pays a dividend, this date is important: If you buy on or after the ex-dividend date, you aren't entitled to a dividend. The coffee company has never paid a dividend and "presently intends to retain earnings to help finance the company's continued growth." (Investor Relations, Investor Frequently Asked Questions, www.starbucks.com)

Coffee Quiz

MOST OF THE WORLD'S COFFEE IS GROWN BETWEEN WHAT TWO REGIONS?

Hint: Think back to geography class and decide what rings a bell.

    a. The Tropic of Cancer and the Tropic of Capricorn
    b. The Equator and the Tropic of Capricorn
    c. The Coffee Region and the Tea Region
    d. The Tropic of Coffee and the Tropic of Tea

Answer: If you guessed "a. The Tropic of Cancer and the Tropic of Capricorn," you are correct. Furthermore, coffee is grown in three main regions located there: Latin America, Asia/Pacific, and Africa/Arabia.

COMMODITY PRICE RISK

Starbucks uses two major commodities—coffee and milk. The price and availability of these commodities can impact operations and the bottom line. The company sells whole-bean and ground coffee, along with utilizing coffee in a number of prepared drinks. So when the price of coffee goes up, it can be a problem for coffee companies like Starbucks. Starbucks also pays a premium for the high-quality arabica coffee it utilizes. The company is fairly successful, however, at locking into contracts and hedging its risks. According to the 10-K for fiscal 2008, the company has good relations with suppliers—coffee producers, outside trading companies, and exporters—so the risk of nondelivery on commitments is small. The good news for Starbucks and its shareholders is that the company's recent 10-K report for the 13 weeks ending December 28, 2008, reported that there had been no material change in the commodity price risk. Commodity price risk represents the company's primary market risk, generated by its purchases of green coffee beans.

The company also purchases significant amounts of dairy products to support its retail stores' needs. U.S. dairy prices rose in 2007 and saw another significant increase in 2008, adversely affecting the U.S. segment and company profitability. This concern over rising milk prices has since subsided, and in early 2009, dairy prices were even falling. In the United States, Starbucks purchases virtually all of its fluid milk from three dairy suppliers. The company maintains that the risk of the milk not being delivered is remote. And Starbucks made a switch from whole milk to 2 percent milk as a standard for its espresso-based drinks in its U.S. and Canadian stores in 2007. Lowfat 2 percent milk is not only healthier, but it is also less expensive—a good health move and also a good cost-cutting move.

Caffeine Kick

According to Starbucks Coffee Company's *Nutrition by the Cup*, based on the company's standard brewing methods, an espresso contains 75 milligrams of caffeine per shot (1 fluid ounce), and brewed coffee contains 20 milligrams of caffeine per fluid ounce.

FOCUS ON THE FUTURE

As Starbucks looks ahead, one keystone it can build on is its well-known concern about the communities that support its stores and also about the broader world community. Ultimately, this will be a positive for the company's future survival. In good economic times or bad, Starbucks makes it a mission to be a socially conscious company through which customers can get involved in helping some great causes. Drink a cup of coffee, it says, and make the world a better place. Starbucks makes it clear: It is a down-to-earth company and is here for the long run. Check out some of the recent programs—and these are just a few of many examples—that keep the coffee giant in touch, involved, and at the forefront of global assistance efforts.

(Product) RED

Through (Product) RED, Starbucks is providing its customers with an opportunity to participate in helping save lives in Africa, which is a key coffee-growing region for the company. Starbucks currently buys coffee from a host of African countries, including Burundi, Cameroon, the Congo, Ethiopia, Kenya, Malawi, Rwanda, Tanzania, Uganda, and Zambia. Recently, Starbucks announced a multiyear partnership with (RED), a business model created to raise awareness and money for AIDS programs in Africa. Between November 27, 2008, and January 2, 2009, Starbucks contributed five cents from each sale of a (RED) drink—espresso truffle, gingersnap latte, or peppermint mocha twist—to the Global Fund. According to the (Product) RED Web site, www.joinred.com, an estimated 4,100 people die every day in Africa because they cannot afford to buy the medicine they need. The relevance of the name (RED) is that red is the color of emergency. A Starbucks press release dated December 18, 2008, reported on the huge impact the company was making. "In just over two weeks since these products were introduced, Starbucks customers have generated contributions equal to more than 1.4 million daily doses of antiretroviral medicine. This equates to providing lifesaving antiretroviral therapy to more than 3,800 people with HIV in Africa for one year."

In 2006, famous U2 singer Bono cofounded (RED), which develops cobranded (RED) products with companies such as American Express, Apple, Converse, Dell, Emporio Armani, Gap, Hallmark, and Microsoft—with a portion of the profits from each (RED) product going to benefit the Global Fund, the dominant financer of programs to fight AIDS, tuberculosis, and malaria around the world. Bono appeared at the Starbucks leadership conference in New Orleans in late October 2008 to announce the partnership with (RED). Starting on January 3, 2009, and continuing through the end of 2009, Starbucks committed to contribute five cents from every purchase made with a Starbucks Card to its (RED) campaign.

Starbucks Supports Communities

As a way to start off the 2008 school year, and in recognition of teachers, Starbucks offered teachers of kindergarten through 12th grade a complimentary tall-size cup of brewed Pike Place Roast every Monday during September at U.S. stores. Starbucks asked teachers to simply provide proof of current teacher status, such as a teachers' federation card or a school district badge. This was part of a program titled Great Start for Great Teachers.

Educators play an essential role in the future of communities everywhere. This promotion was one way for Starbucks to say thank you and to recognize teachers for their significant contribution of time and expertise to the young people of America. One of the reasons Starbucks is the global coffee giant it has become is that the company is smart. Not only is a program like this a nice thing to do, it generates goodwill between the company and communities and also brings teachers, who may be new customers, into stores. Once they are inside, they might decide to buy an extra pound or two of coffee to take home. And once they visit their local Starbucks, chances are they will be back. Cool idea, cool marketing!

Starbucks Creates Jobs and Does Right for the Environment

Starbucks now has five roasting plants. Its newest and smallest facility opened in February 2009 in Sandy Run, South Carolina. The 120,000-square-foot facility, located in Calhoun County in central South Carolina, joins Starbucks' other four roasting plants, which are located in Kent, Washington; York, Pennsylvania; Carson Valley, Nevada; and Amsterdam, the Netherlands. York is the biggest of its roasting plants and boasts 700,000 square feet. The new South Carolina plant is the smallest facility, because, unlike the other plants, it doesn't distribute noncoffee goods, such as brewing machines and merchandise.

The $70 million roasting facility employs 100 full-time workers and will more efficiently distribute coffee to Starbucks stores in the southeastern United States. According to the Web edition of *The State*, South Carolina's largest newspaper, "Every day, coffee beans from around the world arrive at the plant in 125-pound burlap bags. The beans are shipped to the Port of Charleston and stored in a warehouse in Summerville until they are needed at the roasting plant in Sandy Run. Once the beans arrive in Sandy Run, Starbucks partners—as the company refers to its workers—rip open the burlap bags and pour the beans into a pit. There, debris is shaken out and the beans are stored in silos." The February 20, 2009, article notes that the roasters resemble large dryers, with beans roasting at temperatures above 400°F. Each roasting cycle runs for 12 minutes.

The plant is a LEED (Leadership in Energy and Environmental Design) silver-certified facility, a certification awarded by the U.S. Green Building Council. The plant meets a standard for green design elements for new construction, which reduces energy and waste. Roughly 20 percent of the building materials were made from recycled content, and over 75 percent of construction waste was recycled. The facility has top-notch efficient lighting and water fixtures and drought-tolerant landscaping. Wind will even power a portion of the facility's operations. Starbucks has noted that it will get LEED certification for all new company-operated stores by the end of 2010. Seattle's Starbucks Center, headquarters for the company, has already received the LEED gold certification. Built in 1912, and at over 1,500,000 square feet, Seattle's Starbucks Center is the largest and oldest structure in the country to earn a national green certification for existing buildings, according to the *Seattle Post-Intelligencer* (P-I Staff, "Seattle's Starbucks Center Earns National Green Certification," November 1, 1007).

"During these challenging economic times, I'm proud we are creating jobs by building something special here in South Carolina," Howard Schultz, Starbucks' top man, said in a company press release dated February 19, 2009. "In this business climate, it's more important than ever that we make the right investments in our business, while making sure we do it in ways that support our business, the communities we work in, the environment, and our people."

With a recession going on and unemployment at a 25-year high (the jobless rate hit 9.4 percent in May 2009), the jobs created by Starbucks are no doubt an added boon to the South Carolina economy. There are a total of 12.5 million unemployed people in the nation, so Starbucks' employment stimulation is well appreciated by those who work at the new plant.

Call for National Service

The company is always thinking ahead. In this case, it is looking to the future of our society. Starbucks recently launched its "I'm In!" campaign, an initiative to assist Americans in participating in President Obama's call for national service. The coffee company is partnering with HandsOn Network, a national nonprofit whose goal is to boost volunteerism and inspire Americans to take action that changes the world. The timing of the initiative coincided with President Obama's inauguration, a great moment to encourage a renewed national commitment to service.

At participating Starbucks stores across the nation, customers were invited to pick up pledge cards. As a thank-you gift, Starbucks honored each person who pledged five hours of service with a free tall brewed coffee during a one-week period in January. Customers could choose a local volunteer opportunity of their choice. Just think of the powerful impact even one volunteer could make—spending five hours serving meals at a homeless shelter, or two hours volunteering at the senior citizen shelter and three hours at a crisis nursery, or an hour a day for one week in different divisions of the local library. Starbucks is a catalyst, in that it has access to millions of customers—potential volunteers who can pledge service to their communities. The company's goal was to raise service pledges in excess of a million hours from all over the country. Log on to www.pledge5. starbucks.com to see a running total of hours pledged. At the time of this writing Starbucks had far exceeded the goal with 1.3 million hours and counting.

ECONOMIC CHALLENGES

On January 28, 2009, Starbucks released its first-quarter fiscal 2009 earnings. (See the box labeled Starbucks First-Quarter Fiscal 2009 Financial Results.) In a nutshell, the company posted a net income of $64.3 million—down a staggering 69 percent from the $208.1 million reported one year earlier. Earnings per share for the first quarter of fiscal 2009 were $0.09, and non-GAAP EPS was $0.15, compared with a reported EPS of $0.28 in the first quarter of fiscal 2008. Consolidated net revenues were $2.62 billion for the first quarter of fiscal 2009, a decrease of 6 percent when compared with $2.77 billion for the first quarter of fiscal 2008, driven by a decline in comparable store sales at Starbucks of 9 percent. Store traffic is down, and the value per transaction is down, too.

This is not a very rosy earnings report for the coffee giant. But Starbucks CEO Schultz and his management team aim to address the problems head-on. During times of recession, businesses, retailers, and restaurants across the board struggle for customer dollars. The Starbucks team has a plan of action to cut costs and position itself for longevity as we all dig out of the battered economy. Due to cost restructuring, Starbucks posted its first quarterly loss since going public (a net loss of $6.7 million) in the third quarter of fiscal 2008. Tightening one's belt does not come without pain.

Starbucks First-Quarter Fiscal 2009 Financial Results
First Quarter Ending December 28, 2008 (13 weeks ended)
Consolidated Net Revenues: $2.62 billion
Net Income: $64.3 million
Earnings Per Share: $0.09
Store Total: 16,875

First Quarter Ending December 30, 2007 (13 weeks ended)
Consolidated Net Revenues: $2.77 billion
Net Income: $208.1 million
Earnings Per Share: $0.28
Store Total: 15,756

Source: News release, "Starbucks Reports First Quarter Fiscal 2009 Results," January 28, 2009

"In the midst of the weakening global consumer environment, Starbucks is following a well-developed plan to strengthen our business through more efficient operations and by preserving the fundamental strengths and values of our brand," Schultz commented. "We remain focused on driving the discipline and rigor necessary to create long-term shareholder value, and we are taking aggressive steps to excite customers by providing relevant value and innovation, even during this challenging time."

In the January 2009 press release, Starbucks also addressed the actions that would return the company to sound footing:

Starbucks planned to close 300 underperforming stores, 200 of them in the United States and 100 abroad. These store closings are in addition to the approximately 600 domestic and 61 Australian store closures announced in

July 2008. It was anticipated that the majority of new store closures would be completed by the end of the company's 2009 fiscal year. At the end of 2007, the company had 15,756 stores worldwide. At the end of calendar year 2008, the total number was 16,875 stores across the globe.

The coffee company also said it would scale back on its plans for opening new stores in fiscal 2009, anticipating 140 new stores domestically, from a previous target of 200. Internationally, Starbucks now planned to open 170 new stores in fiscal 2009, down from a previous goal of 270 new stores.

At the time of the announcement, Starbucks employed roughly 167,000 partners at the retail store level, and as many as 6,000 store positions were up for cuts throughout fiscal 2009, due to the likely store closures, decreased store openings, and other labor efficiencies. Whenever possible, the company said, it would move employees to other positions within the organization. In addition, Starbucks planned to cut approximately 700 nonretail workers in the United States and internationally in the weeks following the announcement, including about 350 people at the Starbucks Support Center in Seattle. These cuts were completed by mid-February 2009.

These steps would increase Starbucks' fiscal 2009 cost-savings goals to a targeted level of $500 million (from an earlier goal of $400 million).

Other recent cost-savings cuts and value-adding initiatives included the following:

- Howard Schultz requested that the board cut his salary. His base pay was to be reduced from $1.2 million to $10,000, including health care and other benefits.
- Starbucks made plans to sell two of the three company jets. That included a new $45 million Gulfstream jet that was delivered in December 2008.
- The company decided to expand franchise opportunities for Seattle's Best Coffee to offer café opportunities in the U.S. market.
- Responding to a depressed economy, Starbucks began offering food pairings of coffee and a breakfast item for $3.95, starting in March 2009. This is likely to stir interest in Starbucks, often referenced as the home of $4 coffee, among the economy-minded.
- The company has cut back on all-day brewing of decaffeinated coffee. Afternoon customers now must request decaf, as too many pots of coffee were being wasted after noon, when decaf consumption seems to fall. Customers may have to wait four minutes or so for their decaf order as it is freshly brewed.
- The organization will try to renegotiate more favorable store leases with landlords.

The company reports good progress on its cost-reduction initiatives. Star-bucks announced that cost-cutting measures yielded a benefit of approx-imately $75 million in the first fiscal quarter and are expected to yield approximately $100 million in the second quarter, $150 million in the third quarter, and $175 million in the fourth quarter of fiscal 2009.

SEATTLE'S BEST COFFEE OFFERS FRANCHISES

Seattle's Best Coffee roasts and distributes coffee, along with operating cafes. The company has more than 550 shops, the majority of which are inside Borders bookstores via an in-store licensing program. The coffee is available nationwide in supermarkets and at more than 6,000 food-service locations, such as colleges, restaurants, hotels, airlines, and cruise ships. Founded in 1970, Seattle's Best Coffee was purchased by Starbucks in 2003. At the time of purchase, Seattle's Best Coffee had 129 stores. The brand is well known to customers for having a smoother coffee flavor profile than Starbucks. It offers milder coffee blends and flavored coffees, along with tea, specialty drinks, and food items.

A franchise is a business authorized to sell or distribute a company's goods or services in a particular area. Plain and simple, Starbucks does not franchise. In certain situations, however, Starbucks may consider licensing its operations to companies that can provide improved access to sought-after real estate, such as airports, grocery chains, major food-service corporations, college campuses, and hospitals, among others. Case in point—while Seattle's Best is found in Borders bookstores, Star-bucks has contracted with Barnes & Noble Booksellers' cafes to sell its coffee there.

Starbucks has always wanted its stores controlled at the company level. Seattle's Best Coffee, on the other hand, has a different strategy. After nearly 40 years of nurturing the brand, Seattle's Best Coffee wants to grow by franchising. Seattle's Best Coffee is offering franchises to qualified and select applicants. The company is so serious, it is making franchise infor-mation downloads available on its Web site, www.seattlesbest.com. Check it out and you will find a multitude of information, along with a franchise café brochure, titled Seattle's Best Coffee Franchise Opportunities. The company is using a predefined set of criteria and focusing on multiunit franchisees. Seattle's Best Coffee notes that it is interested in franchisees with a proven track record of success. So, while Starbucks is reducing its number of retail stores in these hard economic times, subsidiary Seattle's Best Coffee is going for the gusto and growing via franchising. Remember, though, that what is good for Seattle's Best Coffee is not always good for Starbucks.

Seattle's Best Coffee prefers franchisees with experience, an under-standing of the food-and-beverage industry, and current ownership of other franchises. "The world of premium coffee has expanded, and customers now expect a great cup of coffee wherever they are," said Tom Ehlers, vice president and general manager of Seattle's Best Coffee, in a press release dated February 19, 2009. "We're excited that by offering a comprehensive franchise program we're able to grow the Seattle's Best Coffee brand, allowing us to fulfill the needs of more specialty coffee customers." As noted in the franchising brochure, the specialty coffee business had total sales of $13.5 billion in the United States in 2007, according to the Specialty Coffee Association of America. Additionally, it noted, coffeehouse sales are predicted to increase 125 percent between 2005 and 2010, according to Mintel's Coffehouses and Donut Shops Report. Interested individuals may indeed want to investigate this fast-paced and growing business opportunity.

The Seattle's Best franchise program will initially focus its efforts on western states and Texas. However, it will consider inquiries from those wanting to start stores anywhere in the nation. Seattle's Best Coffee has access to real estate in markets that might be of interest and might provide an attractive opportunity to qualified franchisees.

According to the *Seattle Times*, launching a Seattle's Best Coffee café runs $298,000 to $481,500 for a storefront, or $191,000 to $521,000 for a kiosk. The royalty is 7 percent, which means a franchisee would pay 7 percent of all revenues to Seattle's Best Coffee.

NEW PRODUCT INNOVATION

Starbucks coffeehouses do keep up with the times. Case in point—the recent emphasis on handcrafted tea beverages and coffee in instant form. It's hard to imagine that tea could rev up the financials at the mega coffeehouse, but it is indeed tea time at Starbucks. In a press release dated December 30, 2008, Michelle Gass, executive vice president of marketing and category, explained:

> In fact, tea is the most consumed beverage around the world and represents one in ten beverages consumed in our stores. The same way we transformed American coffee culture, we want to deliver an exceptional tea experience for customers with our new Tazo Tea Lattes and Tea Infusions.

On January 3, 2009, Starbucks began selling three new tea-based lattes made with steamed milk and Tazo tea, along with two nondairy tea beverages. All the drinks are part of the company's commitment to provide customers with healthier choices. Most of the tea beverages have less than 200 calories for a tall size of 12 ounces and are packed with antioxidants.

Starbucks also announced its latest innovation—instant coffee—in a February 12, 2009, press release. The instant coffee, Starbucks VIA Ready Brew, will be sold in packages of three servings for $2.95, or 12 packages for $9.95. For the economy-minded consumer, that means you can get a cup of Starbucks coffee for less than $1. Now, that is an affordable treat for most people. The soluble-coffee product aims to appeal to a wider group of coffee consumers—both the economy-minded and those interested in a quick single serving at home—but will still have the quality Starbucks taste. It has been in development for more than 20 years, and Starbucks maintains that it replicates the "body and flavor of Starbucks coffee in instant form" (New Release: "Starbucks VIA Ready Brew: A Breakthrough in Instant Coffee," February 17, 2009). Starbucks VIA Ready Brew can be made by adding either hot or cold water.

VIA was made available in some Starbucks cafés in Seattle, the Chicago area, and London as of March 2009. The instant beverage can also be ordered online at www.StarbucksVIA.com. The instant coffee will be available across the United States by fall 2009. Schultz said, "This is a big move for us—the opportunity to reinvent a category, create new rituals, and grow our customer base is substantial" (News Release: "Starbucks VIA Ready Brew: A Breathrough in Instant Coffee," February 17, 2009). Instant coffee is a $17 billion global market, and one that Starbucks is smart to get into its game plan.

YOU DECIDE

To Franchise or Not to Franchise?

Starbucks has always taken a stand against franchising its stores. The coffeehouses were exclusively company owned until Starbucks started considering a few licensing agreements in more recent years. If you were a Starbucks executive, what would you say? Is franchising good for a company? What are the pros and cons? And what's the difference between licensing and franchising? If you'd like to find out more about it, you could go to www.seattlesbestcoffee.com and download information on the For Business pages about both options to compare.

STILL THE PREMIUM RETAILER

Starbucks built its success on using high-quality arabica coffee beans, in lieu of commercially mass-produced coffee. And Starbucks is not willing to give up its promise of exceptional taste in its fine coffees, teas, specialty drinks, and food products. It may be a small luxury, but loyal Starbucks customers have not been deterred, even in hard economic times. Until the economy rebounds, the financial picture for Starbucks may be murky. But as the economy strengthens, Starbucks is likely to emerge as a stronger operator, more in tune with consumers. Do you want a $4 gourmet coffee beverage or a $1 instant brew? Starbucks has shown it can excel at either. The company is striving to reinvigorate the brand and still remain king of the premium coffee industry. Starbucks *is* the number one gourmet specialty coffee retailer in the world!

TOP TEN REASONS STARBUCKS IS THE COFFEE KING

1. **Howard Schultz**—The company's top man is a visionary and great leader who understands the changing coffee environment.
2. **Ability to pinch pennies**—There is strong evidence Starbucks can be budget-minded by reducing costs and closing underperforming stores to increase efficiency.
3. **Quality coffee = a great product**—Exceptional arabica coffee, along with other food and beverage items, is a desired product that people will continue to consume for the long term.
4. **Strong brand name**—Starbucks is associated with superiority, and the company can charge a premium for excellence.
5. **Great customers, partners, and community relations**—The ongoing support of customers, employees, and local communities will keep the company moving forward.
6. **Policies that favor coffee farmers**—Starbucks supports sustainability to help coffee farmers thrive, which is mutually beneficial.
7. **Environmentally friendly decision making**—Starbucks is a green company and works to minimize its environmental footprint.
8. **Healthier food and drink options**—The company has shown that it is sensitive to America's concerns about a healthier lifestyle.
9. **An open ear for customers**—Open dialogue at www.mystarbucksidea.com is a great vehicle for customers to suggest ideas, and the company has shown that it honestly considers them.
10. **International expansion**—Overseas growth is young, and opportunities are boundless.

Starbucks through the Decades: A Timeline to Success

1971   Jerry Baldwin, Gordon Bowker, and Zev Siegl open the first Starbucks Coffee, Tea, and Spices store in the trendy Seattle Pike Place Market. The original purpose of the store is to sell gourmet coffee beans, along with coffee-related merchandise and equipment. They occasionally offer brewed samples, but just for tasting.

1972   The second Starbucks Coffee store opens in Seattle.

1980   Siegl decides he wants to leave Starbucks and pursue other interests. He sells out his interest to Baldwin and Bowker.

1982   Howard Schultz joins the company as director of retail operations and marketing.

1983   Schultz travels to Milan, Italy, for Starbucks to attend an international housewares show. He visits and is impressed with Milan's espresso bars and sees the potential to develop a similar Italian-style coffee culture for Starbucks.

1984   Baldwin and Bowker purchase Peet's Coffee & Tea. Schultz tries to convince the founders that the coffee bar concept is right for Starbucks, but the original duo holds on to the vision of the company as a retailer of quality coffee beans and not in the beverage business. Schultz finally persuades the founders to allow him to put the coffeehouse concept to a test in a downtown Seattle store, where the espresso bar concept is embraced by customers.

1985   Unable to get further support of his coffee bar idea from the original founders, Schultz leaves to start up his own company—Il Giornale, an Italian-style coffeehouse. Il Giornale offers brewed coffee and espresso beverages made from Starbucks coffee beans.

1987   Baldwin and Bowker sell Starbucks—the six Seattle stores, the roasting plant, and the Starbucks name—keeping only the Peet's assets. Il Giornale, along with some local investors, acquires the Starbucks assets and changes its name to Starbucks Corporation. Schultz returns to Starbucks as president and CEO. A new

Starbucks is born! The first stores are opened outside of Seattle, in Chicago and Vancouver, British Columbia.

*By the end of 1987, Starbucks has grown to 17 stores.

1988   Starbucks offers part-time employees working 20 or more hours the same health coverage as full-timers.

1991   Credit Starbucks with a major first! Starbucks becomes the first private company to offer a company-wide stock option plan that includes part-time workers. The plan is cleverly dubbed Bean Stock. Starbucks also opens its first licensed airport store.

1992   Starbucks goes public with an initial public offering (IPO), becoming the first specialty coffee company to do so. The company's common stock is traded on the NASDAQ under the trading symbol SBUX.

*At the end of fiscal year 1992, the company has a total of 165 stores, but the growth is just beginning.

1993   Starbucks opens a second roasting facility in Kent, Washington. Starbucks also broadens its interests by entering into a relationship with Barnes & Noble Booksellers to serve its gourmet coffee in B&N bookstore coffee shops—the first of many partnerships of this sort.

1995   Starbucks starts selling music compilations on compact discs. The company also begins serving Frappuccino blended beverages and enters into an agreement with Dreyer's Grand Ice Cream to produce a super-premium line of ice cream. It is awarded an account with United Airlines and opens a third roasting plant in York, Pennsylvania.

1996   Another first for the company, Starbucks International introduces its first stores outside of North America, in Tokyo and Singapore. Starbucks and Pepsi-Cola Company begin a business venture called the North American Coffee Partnership to sell a bottled version of Starbucks Frappuccino blended coffee beverages. Starbucks' new line of super-premium ice cream hits supermarket shelves.

*At fiscal year-end 1996, the company store count tops the 1,000 mark, totaling 1,015.

1997   CEO Schultz donates the proceeds from his book, *Pour Your Heart into It*, in order to establish the Starbucks Foundation. Contributions from the foundation benefit local literacy programs in communities where Starbucks has coffeehouses.

1998   The company launches Starbucks.com. Starbucks announces plans to sell coffee in supermarkets nationwide through an agreement with Kraft. The company enters the UK market by acquiring the Seattle Coffee Company in the United Kingdom, with more than 60 stores.

1999   Starbucks buys Tazo, a tea company based in Portland, Oregon. The company also purchases a San Francisco-based music company called Hear Music. Starbucks begins a partnership with Conservation International to promote methods of coffee growing that are environmentally responsible.

*At fiscal year-end 1999, the company store total is 2,498.

2000   Orin Smith is promoted to president and CEO of the company. Schultz transitions from chairman and CEO to chairman and chief global strategist. Starbucks establishes a licensing agreement with TransFair USA to sell Fair Trade Certified coffee in the United States and Canada. Starbucks introduces Fair Trade Certified coffee to its product line and purchases 190,000 pounds of Fair Trade Certified coffee. Starbucks begins its Grounds for Your Garden coffee grounds recycling and conservation program on a national basis.

*At the end of fiscal year 2000, the company store total hits 3,501.

2001   Starbucks begins to offer high-speed wireless Internet access in select stores. The Starbucks Card is unveiled—a prepaid purchasing card that customers can use and reload. The Starbucks Foundation signs on for a four-year, $1 million philanthropic partnership with Jumpstart, a national organization that pairs college student tutors with preschoolers. Starbucks provides $1 million in financial support to coffee farmers through Calvert Community Investments. The company develops its socially responsible coffee buying guidelines called C.A.F.E. (Coffee and Farmer Equity) Practices.

*At fiscal year-end 2001, the company store total is 4,709.

2002   The company publishes its first Corporate Social Responsibility (CSR) report. The Starbucks "Make Your Mark" program begins to organize volunteers and contribute time and money to North American charitable organizations.

*At fiscal year-end 2002, the company store total tops the 5,000 mark—5,886 Starbucks stores.

2003   Starbucks acquires the U.S.–based Seattle Coffee Company, which includes the Seattle's Best Coffee and Torrefazione Italia coffee brands. The deal total is $72 million in cash. The company also opens new roasting facilities in Carson Valley, Nevada, and overseas in Amsterdam, the Netherlands. Starbucks continues its commitment to literacy programs and community youth and educational organizations.

*At fiscal year-end 2003, the company store count totals 7,225.

2004   Tazo and Kraft Foods announce a licensing agreement to distribute Tazo super-premium teas in U.S. grocery channels. The first Starbucks workers union is formed. The company introduces the Starbucks Coffee Master Program for partners to gain more expertise about the world of coffee. Starbucks releases *Ray Charles, Genius Loves Company* through a collaboration between Concord Records and Hear Music. Starbucks gives money to the Verde Ventures fund and also to Calvert Community Investments, helping these organizations provide affordable credit to small coffee producers and farmers. Starbucks also joins the United Nations Global Compact, for improved environment, labor, and human rights.

*At fiscal year-end 2004, the company store total is up to 8,569.

2005   Orin Smith retires as Starbucks president and CEO. Jim Donald is promoted to president and CEO. *Ray Charles, Genius Loves Company* wins eight Grammy Awards, including Album of the Year and Record of the Year. Starbucks purchases EthosWater, with the goal of donating $10 million to support clean-water projects worldwide by 2010. Starbucks makes its first voyage into international literacy by pledging $5 million to support educational programs in China. It also donates millions of dollars to help victims of Hurricane Katrina and to aid tsunami relief and recovery in South Asia.

*At fiscal year-end 2005, the company store count tops the 10,000 mark, with a total of 10,241.

2006   Starbucks signs a distribution agreement with the North American Coffee Partnership to distribute EthosWater. Starbucks becomes the first company in the United States to use 10 percent post-consumer fiber (PCF) in its hot-beverage cups. To celebrate Starbucks' 35-year anniversary, the company's first downloadable audio program series, *Coffee Conversations*, educates customers about the world of coffee.

*At fiscal year-end 2006, the company store total hits 12,440.

2007   Starbucks converts to 2 percent milk as its beverage standard in the United States and Canada. Store traffic slows. Starbucks' Hear Music signs Paul McCartney as the first artist to record with the new label.

*At fiscal year-end 2007, the company store total tops the 15,000 mark—an amazing 15,756 stores worldwide.

2008   Donald is out as head of the company, and Schultz returns as CEO to mend the financially troubled coffeehouse. Starbucks announces it will close approximately 600 U.S. stores as a step in improving the company's long-term profitable growth. Starbucks is ranked number 17 on the U.S. Environmental Protection Agency's Top 50 Green

Power Partners list for purchases of renewable energy. Starbucks' Great Start for Great Teachers program offers a complimentary tall (12-ounce) cup of Pike Place Roast every Monday throughout the month of September to teachers of kindergarten through 12th grade. Starbucks partners with Hershey to offer Starbucks chocolate, to be sold at mass retailers, grocery stores, and drugstores. Starbucks tests $1 short (8-ounce) brewed coffees in Seattle. Signature Hot Chocolate is introduced. Starbucks takes numerous steps toward offering healthier options, including five new permanent healthier breakfast choices. The company launches its first online suggestion Web site at www.mystarbucksidea.com, an online community for customer input. Starbucks contributes five cents from the sale of each (RED)-branded holiday drink—espresso truffle, gingersnap latte, or peppermint mocha twist—to the Global Fund, investing in programs dealing with the AIDS epidemic in Africa. Wireless communication between Apple Inc.'s iTunes and select Starbucks stores becomes available through AT&T Wi-Fi. In July, the company announces the closing of approximately 600 U.S. stores and 61 Australian stores. The company's 10-K report, filed with the U.S. Securities and Exchange Commission, looks ahead and calls fiscal 2009 "extremely challenging."

*At fiscal year-end 2008, the company store total is up over the 16,000 mark—16,680.

2009   Starbucks opens its fifth roasting plant in Sandy Run, South Carolina. New tea beverages are introduced. Starbucks launches its "I'm In!" campaign, helping answer President Obama's call for national service. The company introduces its latest innovation, Starbucks VIA—a breakthrough in instant coffee. The (RED) campaign continues, with Starbucks contributing five cents from every purchase made with a Starbucks customer rewards card beginning in January. A company announcement increases the company's fiscal 2009 cost-reduction target from $400 million to $500 million. Efforts include closing 300 more stores and reducing employees by 6,700.

Sources: Personal research, including data obtained from press releases, and Company Timeline, available at www.starbucks.com.

Appendix B

The Futures of Coffee

The Coffee, Sugar, and Cocoa Exchange is now part of the Intercontinental Exchange (ICE) Futures U.S. in New York, as of 2007. It dates from 1882, when the Coffee Exchange of New York was established for merchants and traders. The coffee C Contract is the world benchmark market pricing for arabica coffee, and the coffee industry views the C Contract as a guide to the cost of business. Starbucks buys very little coffee from the exchange, though, and prefers to buy what it considers a high-quality grade directly from farmers.

The contract price includes physical delivery of the coffee, although it is largely used for hedging, with no physical delivery actually made. Only about 1 percent of transactions results in physical delivery from a supplier to a roaster or manufacturer. And you'd better know what you are buying, because if you do take delivery, a C Contract is for 37,500 pounds of coffee—enough to fill an entire truckload. Big companies that are highly competitive on price do buy here, trying to get coffee at the lowest price possible.

The Exchange uses select coffees from Mexico, El Salvador, Guatemala, Costa Rica, Nicaragua, Kenya, New Guinea, Panama, Tanzania, Uganda, Honduras, and Peru to establish the basis for the C contract. Colombian coffee brings in a premium over the basis, and coffees judged of lesser quality from Venezuela, Burundi, India, Rwanda, the Dominican Republic, and Ecuador trade at a discount from the basis. Price differentials are determined based on quality of the beans, and traders buy and sell against those prices.

The contract prices physical delivery of exchange-grade green beans, from one of 19 countries of origin. A price quote is listed, for example, at 136.20 cents per pound, or $1.362 per pound. The C Contract is forced up or down due to supply-and-demand shifts, including unexpected weather conditions, such as a drought or flood; political turmoil or war; economic instability; and other unpredictable factors. Because Starbucks buys top-quality coffee, it typically pays a price above the C. But when the C skyrockets, so does the price of coffee for Starbucks. It is a basic economic indicator for the company.

THE C CONTRACT

Historically, weather fluctuations, long sea routes in trade, and imbalances of supply and demand caused huge variation in coffee pricing—so much so that in 1880, cash speculation in coffee caved the market. In an effort to bring some order to pricing in the coffee market, importers and dealers met in lower Manhattan on March 7, 1882, to trade in coffee futures. The first transaction on the New York Coffee Exchange was for 250 bags of coffee. A spokesperson from the ICE Futures U.S. in New York, where coffee is now traded, pointed out some of the details of trading this volatile commodity:

What Is the Coffee C Contract? What Is the Contract Size?

The contract calls for delivery of 37,500 pounds of arabica coffee in any one of several delivery points; full contract specifications are at www.theice.com/publicdocs/futures_us/Coffee_Fact_Sheet.pdf.

What Percentage of Traders Actually Take Physical Delivery of Coffee?

Less than half of 1 percent of positions are held until the expiration of the futures contract and taken to delivery.

Why Is There Volatility in the Coffee Market?

As with other products, coffee prices are determined by supply-and-demand factors. Supply in particular is not constant, as the crop can be significantly increased by favorable weather and significantly decreased by unfavorable weather. This surely contributes to price volatility in the coffee market.

Explain What Type of People (or Businesses) Might Be Interested in Coffee Contracts.

We generally divide traders of any of our products into two classes: *hedgers*, which in the coffee market would include producers, roasters, and merchant firms that help move the product from origin to end user and that therefore hold long inventories and also have sales commitments not offset by inventory held; and *speculators*, including individual speculators, funds, index investors, and so on.

Appendix C

Glossary of Coffee Terms

Acidity The quality that makes coffee sharp and refreshing. A tangy taste experienced mainly on the edges of your tongue and at the back of the palate. Coffee needs a level of acidity; otherwise, it will taste flat. As the roast develops, the coffee acidity falls.

Aftertaste The sensation of coffee vapors that remains in your mouth after swallowing.

Americano A style of coffee made by combining hot water with espresso. The strength of an Americano can vary depending on the amount of water and the amount of espresso added. The strength can be increased by increasing the number of shots of espresso.

Arabica The earliest-cultivated coffee and the most widely grown. It is considered to produce the highest quality of coffee (see *robusta*). This species is grown at higher altitudes and prefers to be grown in shade. The taste is more refined, milder, aromatic, and flavorful. It can be dark-roasted for a bold taste.

Aroma A distinctive, pleasant odor. Aroma involves the art of smelling coffee and is difficult to separate from flavor. It gives you the first hint of how your coffee will taste.

Bag A burlap sack of coffee used to ship the commodity around the globe. Weight may differ by country, but the most common measurement of a bag is 60 kilograms, or 132 pounds.

Balance A coffee quality in which no single characteristic of the coffee overwhelms the others.

Barista A person professionally trained in the art of making espresso. This term is often used to describe someone who is employed to make coffee drinks or work behind the counter of a coffee shop.

Blend The act of combining coffees from different origins. Blending coffee beans is designed to produce a unique, signature taste.

Body The weight or thickness of a coffee brew. This is the sensation of heaviness when one tastes coffee. Examples of body categories are light, medium, and full.

Bouquet The smell of the coffee grounds.

Breve Espresso made with cream.

Brew A drink made by boiling, steeping, or mixing various ingredients.

C contract The C is the world benchmark market pricing for Arabica coffee. Those in the coffee industry view the C contract as a guide to the cost of business.

Caffeine A bitter alkaloid found in coffee, tea, and various other plant parts. It stimulates the central nervous system, causing increased alertness, energy, and attention.

Cappuccino A beverage made from espressò, hot steamed milk, and frothed milk. The drink is typically made with 1/3 espresso, 1/3 steamed milk, and 1/3 frothed milk on top. Sometimes, the frothed milk is sprinkled with cinnamon or powdered chocolate. The drink (Italian for little Capuchin) gets its name from the Capuchin order of Franciscan friars, because the whipped cream rising to a point resembled a friar with his long, pointed brown hood, or *capuche*, pulled up.

Cherry The ripened fruit of the coffee tree. The plant actually resembles a tall bush or shrub. The fruits are referred to as coffee cherries and are bright red when ready to pick. Coffee beans are the pits of the coffee cherry. Most coffee cherries contain two beans, but occasionally (in roughly 5 to 10 percent of fruits) only one bean is produced by a cherry. This single bean is called a peaberry. Coffee cherries are hand-picked by farmers.

Clean A coffee that is free from flavor defects.

Coffee Quality Institute (CQI) A nonprofit organization formed to improve the quality of coffee and the lives of the people who produce it.

Cupping Tasting coffee; a procedure used by professional tasters to test a coffee's quality. Cupping allows one to compare coffee samples with each other.

Dark roast The darkest style of roasting coffee beans that produces a deep, rich, full-bodied cup of coffee.

Decaffeinated Having the caffeine removed; this may apply to coffee, tea, or other products. Decaffeinating coffee is achieved through a variety of decaffeination methods. For those affected negatively by caffeine, decaffeinated (or *decaf*) coffee is an alternative. Almost all brands of decaffeinated coffee still contain some trace levels of caffeine.

Espresso A strong, concentrated coffee made by forcing hot water through finely ground coffee beans under pressure. It is used as a main component for coffee drinks, such as americanos, cappuccinos, and lattes.

Fair-trade coffee Coffee that has been purchased from farmers at a fair, above-market price intended to raise the living standards of small-scale coffee farmers.

Finish The taste that is left on the palate after the coffee is spat out or swallowed.

Flavor A sensory evaluation of coffee after the merging of aroma, acidity, and body.

Fragrance The smell of coffee after the beans have been ground.

Grade The classification of green coffee by size and density of the beans.

Green beans The seeds contained within the coffee fruits that, when roasted and ground, yield coffee. Usually greenish in color, they can range from dull beige to light green, jade, or even blue-green.

Green coffee Raw coffee beans that have not been roasted.

Hard bean Coffee grown at relatively high altitudes—4,000 to 4,500 feet. Coffee grown above 4,500 feet is referred to as strictly hard bean. Beans grown at higher altitudes mature more slowly and are harder and denser than other beans, and thus more desirable.

Instant coffee Brewed coffee that is dehydrated to make it instantly soluble when mixed with hot water.

International Coffee Organization (ICO) The main intergovernmental organization for coffee, founded in London in 1963, in collaboration with the United Nations. The ICO is responsible for addressing the challenges of the global coffee sector through international cooperation. Members include 45 exporting countries, along with 32 importing countries. These exporting members account for more than 97 percent of world coffee production, while importing members account for 80 percent of world coffee consumption.

Java An island of Indonesia that is a big producer of coffee and gave its name to a generic cup of coffee.

Joe A slang name for coffee, after Admiral Josephus "Joe" Daniels, U.S. chief of naval operations, who outlawed alcohol on board ships in 1914 and ordered coffee as the beverage of service; also *cup of joe.*

Latte A coffee beverage made with espresso and topped with steamed milk. Often, the ratio is 1/3 espresso topped with 2/3 steamed milk.

Macchiato Generally speaking, the Italian term means marked. An espresso macchiato is espresso marked with a small amount of foamed milk.

Mocha A type of high-quality coffee bean from Arabia. This term also describes a beverage combining chocolate and a form of coffee, usually espresso.

National Coffee Association (NCA) The National Coffee Association of the USA was founded in 1911 and was the first trade association for the coffee industry in the United States. Its widely referenced *National Coffee Drinking Trends* study has monitored U.S. coffee consumption since 1950. The NCA has promoted the U.S. coffee industry with international trading organizations, along with more than 50 coffee-producing countries. At home, the NCA has represented the U.S. coffee industry within the government, including the U.S. Department of Agriculture, U.S. Trade Representative's Office, U.S. Food and Drug Administration, and Congressional committees.

Nose The sensation of vapors released by the brewed coffee in the mouth.

Organic coffee Produced without the use of synthetic pesticides, herbicides, or chemical fertilizers. To be *certified organic,* farmers must verify that they are using accepted organic practices and undergo soil testing. Certification can therefore be costly and accounts for the higher prices of many organic coffees.

Roast To brown green coffee beans by drying and exposing to heat; the process of transforming green coffee beans into roasted coffee. The darker the roast, the heavier the flavor.

Robusta A poorer quality of coffee and less expensive compared to the superior arabica. Robusta is usually used for lower-quality coffee blends and is utilized in jars of instant coffee and mass supermarket-grade blends. Arabica coffee is generally utilized in coffeehouses and specialty food and grocery stores. Robusta coffee has a high caffeine content, with nearly twice as much caffeine as arabica coffee. Robusta is a hardier coffee plant that is more resistant to weather conditions, has a greater crop yield, and requires less care than arabica. Its taste is harsh.

Shade grown Refers to coffee grown underneath a canopy, often formed by other trees. Contrast this with coffee grown in direct sunlight. Shade-grown coffee implies organic or other ecologically sensitive growing conditions.

Single-origin coffee Coffee from a specific growing region.

Soft bean Describes coffee grown at relatively low altitudes—below 4,000 feet. Coffee plants grown at lower altitudes mature more quickly and produce a lighter, more porous bean.

Specialty coffee Also referred to as gourmet or premium coffee. These coffees are made from superior beans grown in ideal climates. Specialty coffees tend to produce distinctive flavors, unique to the regions in which they were grown.

Specialty Coffee Association of America (SCAA) Headquartered in Long Beach, California, the SCAA was formed in 1982 and is today the world's largest coffee trade association. The most influential and recognized authority on specialty coffee, the association involves more than 3,000 members. These include producers, retailers, roasters, and importers from 40 countries, although the bulk of members are located in the United States.

Tonne A metric ton; the measurement used in coffee shipments.

Whole-bean coffee Roasted coffee, but not ground.

Appendix D

Starbucks Stars, Cool Coffee Web Sites, and Wonderful Webcasts/Podcasts

STARBUCKS STARS

http://news.starbucks.com/

Starbucks recently launched its new Starbucks newsroom, and it definitely gets high marks. Fans of the company can spend hours exploring this well done Web site filled with up-to-date executive bios and photos. Haven't seen a photo of the well-known Howard Schultz? Check out the Web site for a look at the CEO and a glimpse into his first encounter with and vision for Starbucks. The multimedia is jam-packed full of great Starbucks photos and—a favorite of site visitors—video clips. They are clever, catchy and a great introduction to making a perfect cup of coffee. Don't miss the videos prepared by the company introducing its new instant coffee, Starbucks VIA. The News section is top-notch for anyone interested in the company; you can check out current news and even scan a detailed press release archive. And if you just want to learn about the Starbucks Corporation, you can get the 411. About Us will route you to the company mission and a detailed company timeline or take you to the investor relations page, where you can get the financial lowdown. Starbucks, you get an A+ for providing information to the interested and curious!

www.hearmusic.com

It is well worth your time and totally enjoyable to browse through this Web site. Hear Music was founded in 1990 as a catalog company before being purchased by Starbucks in 1999 for a reported $10 million sum. Hear Music is commonly referred to as "The Sound of Starbucks" and has a spectacular online presence. The company's hand-selected and compiled CDs are featured at Starbucks coffeehouses, Starbucks Hear Music stores, and, of course, online. Click on Music and you can get a list of top spins in stores. Browse the Hear Music catalog and you will most likely end up with CDs in your cart you'll want to purchase. For the movie fan, scan Movies and you will locate independent films as well as mainstream motion pictures to buy—a wide variety chosen by Starbucks. Books are another enjoyable companion for your coffee, and Starbucks has chosen a fabulous selection. Sample the video interviews with select authors, helpful in making a decision if the subject matter is your thing and you would enjoy the read. It's totally fun to hit Collections and Barista Beats for a list of top-five music favorites chosen by Starbucks partners from across the globe. Check out Starbucks iTunes, too. Like what you hear playing at your local Starbucks? You don't need to miss a beat. Download the song to your iPhone, iPod Touch, or laptop while you are enjoying your coffee or specialty beverage. Read the Web site for further details.

www.seattlesbest.com

This specialty retailer and wholesaler became part of Starbucks in 2003, and its Web site deserves a look-see. You'll be greeted by a coffee cup inviting you to "Go ahead. Take it for a spin." Accept the challenge and you will be introduced to the Café menu of shakes, blended beverages, mochas, lattes, teas, brewed coffee in 13 blends and varieties, and much more. Take a stroll over all Coffee Blends or check them out in groups labeled bright, balanced, big, or flavored. A favorite—click Helpful Tips for Home Brewing, which gives great recommendations for making a superb cup of coffee. It is coffee education at its best. Among the tips: "The wrong proportion of coffee beans to water can have the same negative effect on the taste of coffee as using an improper grind. Use fewer grounds and your coffee will be weaker; add more grounds and it will be stronger." You can click Video Lounge and see coffee being roasted in the Seattle's Best Coffee Roasting Plant. Check out the green coffee bean before it is roasted. Coffee Farming is equally fascinating, as you can watch the coffee beans being harvested. My favorite is Tasting Coffee, which gives you a quick peek into the eighth-floor tasting room of Seattle's Best Coffee, where company leaders evaluate coffee samples from around the world. You get a super-quick lesson in tasting coffee, called *cupping* by the pros. Try your own coffee tasting and feel like an expert.

www.starbucksfoundation.org

Schultz founded the Starbucks Foundation back in 1997, and it has seen impressive results. Philanthropy is the name of the game, and Schultz initiated the funding of this organization with proceeds from his book, *Pour Your Heart into It* (1997). To date, more than $22 million in grants and benefits have been made available to communities around the world. Click on one of three ongoing programs to find out the exciting details. Hit the Starbucks Social Entrepreneurs Fund and you will be directed to young social entrepreneurs around the world who are creating positive solutions to needs in their neighborhoods. Are you interested in making your community a better place? Get inspiration here—read stories about young people around the world who are making a difference.

You can even share your story to help motivate others. Keep clicking to Organizations for a list of groups that support social entrepreneurs. One example is Hands On, Miami's Youth Volunteer Corps, which engages teenagers in important, rewarding, and meaningful direct service and service-learning projects throughout Miami/Dade County. Another is City at Peace—New York, a nonprofit that empowers teens to create safe, healthy, peaceful lives and communities, helping build the new generation of community leaders in NYC.

Move on to the second area and hit The EthosWater Fund. This Starbucks-owned company, labeled "a brand with a social mission," helps children around the world gain access to clean water. For every bottle sold, a nickel goes to the EthosWater Fund, which is part of the Starbucks Foundation. Starbucks has a goal of donating $10 million to humanitarian water programs by 2010. It is a worthy and substantial goal, and the company has already achieved $6.2 million of it. It is worth your time to enter www.ethoswater.com and click on Who We Help. For example, read about the Spring Water Catchment Program that benefits all 150 residents of Cholusnate, Honduras. In the past, the women and children spent hours every day collecting water, and their lack of sanitation facilities was another notable problem. This program created a clean, potable source of water right outside their homes. Another huge plus for the village—18 household latrines were installed.

Last, look in Supporting Coffee Communities to learn about Starbucks' strong commitment to being a responsible company and its tremendous plans to build up the coffee industry. You can read about the Starbucks Guatemala Education Initiative, a program designed with Save the Children to bring bilingual education to children in the rural coffee farming communities of Guatemala. Starbucks has committed $1.5 million to this worthy project over four years. Poverty in this area is rampant, and education is a proven tool to break the cycle of poverty and improve lives.

This extensive Web site is powerful and inspiring and makes you want to take a cue from the Starbucks Foundation to get out in the world and do great things.

COOL COFFEE WEB SITES

www.scaa.org

The Specialty Coffee Association of America (SCAA) is the world's largest coffee trade association, with more than 3,000 company members, and is headquartered in Long Beach, California. The SCAA offers a variety of membership options for coffee professionals and casual coffee enthusiasts. The mission of the SCAA is to be the recognized authority on specialty coffee, and the Web site is definitely worth investigating. You thought all coffee was the same? Specialty coffee is sometimes called gourmet coffee and has a richer, more balanced flavor than mass-produced, conventional coffee. Specialty coffees are derived from "exceptional beans grown only in ideal coffee-producing climates." (SCAA of America Lounge, "What is Specialty Coffee?") Why drink specialty coffee? SCAA says, "Quite simply, because it tastes better." Coffee is a $12 billion-plus industry and booming—one of the fastest-growing food-service segments in the world. Click on Lounge and you will enter the popular Coffee Lounge to find lots of information about specialty coffee. Take a look at one of the SCAA Fact Sheets, such as Brewing Facts, and you will find there are six essential elements to coffee brewing. Did you know there is a specific coffee-to-water ratio? According to the site, "Because coffee is a strong flavoring agent, it takes relatively little to produce a robust brew. Regardless of brewing method, 7–9 grams of freshly roasted coffee is required to produce a single serving of properly extracted coffee." Keep on clicking to find the other five brewing tips and enjoy the best cup of coffee ever!

www.ico.org

The International Coffee Organization (ICO) was founded in London in 1963 and is the main intergovernmental body of 45 coffee-exporting and 32 coffee-importing countries. Global coffee meetings, events, and conferences—they are all here to see with just a click or two. If you want trade statistics or coffee prices in select countries, you need not look any further. FYI: World production of exporting countries for 2007 was at 118,290,000 bags, with Ethiopia accounting for 5,733,000 bags. Click on Positively Coffee and you will be directed to www.positivelycoffee.org, part of the Positive Communication program of the ICO, which addresses the health and beneficial aspects of drinking coffee. Or go to Coffee and Mental Performance, where I found out that "Coffee helps to improve alertness, attention, and wakefulness, and by that means it facilitates relevant learning." And if you are into heavy reading, you can even access the text of the seventh International Coffee Agreement, from 2007. The goal of the agreement is to promote international cooperation in the trade of coffee and to strengthen the global coffee sector—you can read all 43 pages. If you just can't get enough biology, check out the page on Botanical Aspects of coffee. Coffee belongs to the Rubiaceae family, which has some 500 genera and over 6,000 species. You can learn about the two most important species of this family, Coffea arabica (arabica coffee) and Coffea canephora (robusta coffee). If it is coffee-related around the globe, you can probably find your answer on this highly detailed Web site.

www.ncausa.org

The National Coffee Association (NCA) of U.S.A, Inc., founded in 1911 and based in New York, was the first trade association for the U.S. coffee industry. You can spend hours reading the consumer-friendly All about Coffee section. At your fingertips: The History of Coffee, Ten

Steps to Coffee—from the Seed to the Cup, How to Store Coffee, How to Brew Coffee, Roasting Types, Coffee around the World, and, my personal favorites, Value of Coffee and Coffee Recipes. Here, you will find Ice Cream Parlor Mocha Sodas, Profiteroles with Coffee Rum Sauce, and Almond Coffee Cream—just some of the delicious yet simple coffee dessert recipes you can check out and whip up on your own. I bet you can already taste the coffee treats. Value of Coffee shows that coffee can be a great deal. According to the Web site, on average, you pay less than a dime for each cup of coffee you make at home. That's a java deal that is hard to beat!

www.vanderbilt.edu/ics/

The Vanderbilt Center for Latin American Studies' Institute for Coffee Studies (ICS) is dedicated to investigating the health benefits of coffee, along with its historical, literary, sociological, and economic importance. Quick Links will route you to coffee associations, organizations, and science sources around the globe. For the consumer who is interested in the key benefits of this bean, click on Coffee News for hours of fun intellectual browsing. Or stream a piece from the *Today Show*, "Craving Caffeine: The Anatomy of a Coffee Lover," touting the not-so-bad elements of the caffeine craze. If you hit Home, you will get a current frame of recent articles on the coffee bean. Check out About ICS to read a welcome from Dr. Peter Martin, director of the ICS. He writes, "Many of us have worried that something this good must be bad for you. But the latest scientific evidence indicates that in moderation (2 to 4 cups per day), coffee may offer key health benefits. ICS is the first research institute to study exactly how this may be." Caffeine lovers, read on!

PREMIER PODCASTS/WEBCASTS

www.fromscratchradio.com

Listen to over 30 minutes of interesting Webcasting from the fabulous *From Scratch*, a weekly radio show about the entrepreneurial life aired on select NPR stations. On a broadcast from January 19, 2007, Jessica Harris, producer and host of *From Scratch*, chats with Peter Thum, founder of EthosWater and vice president of Starbucks. Thum details the founding of this mission-minded company. Ethos was founded in 2002 and purchased by Starbucks in 2005, resulting in a much larger distribution channel for this water with an ethical vision. Starbucks donates five cents for every bottle sold toward humanitarian water programs in developing countries, including Honduras and Kenya. The company's current goal is to invest $10 million in such programs by 2010. You can replay this feel-good, insightful interview with Thum by visiting the *From Scratch* Web site.

www.starbucks.com/ourcoffees/coffeeconversations.asp

As part of the celebration of its 35th anniversary, Starbucks produced its first downloadable audio programming series, called *Coffee Conversations*. The series was taped in September 2006 and consists of an introduction, along with three episodes. You can replay them by visiting the Web site and downloading each one. *Coffee Conversations* is hosted by Scott McMartin, Starbucks' director of coffee education, and Aileen Carrell, manager of green coffee sustainability. Special guests pop in to talk coffee, and you can learn a few fun tips from the pros, as well as expand your coffee vocabulary. Listeners are privy to conversations with a variety of interview guests—coffee farmers, Starbucks baristas, a food expert on entertaining with coffee, and a conservation expert who discusses Starbucks' C.A.F.E. Practices. You may not get a coffee degree, but you will definitely expand your coffee knowledge by listening.

www.chainleader.com

Check out Toque Radio's podcasts for *Chain Leader* magazine. The radio station did a series of talks with food-service businesses about their menus, and guess what? In December 2008, it was Starbucks' turn to chat up its food-and-beverage menu. *Chain Leader* contributing editor Monica Rogers spoke with Starbucks senior nutritionist Katie Thomson about the company's menus and recent healthier food options. Thomson clearly knows her Starbucks products; she has been with the company for over three years. Working closely with the product development and marketing teams, she identifies opportunities for new food-and-beverage products. Thomas then provides recommendations for nutrient levels and ingredients. Listen to the interview: It is evidence she loves her job and the company's products. Thomson remarks, "With beverages, I think our core ingredients—our coffee, tea, and milk—are really a nutritionist's dream, to be honest." If you are interested in Starbucks' nutritional guidelines, menus, healthier food options, and a hint to the direction of products in the future, listen to the great directed queries by Rogers on this taste bud–tempting podcast.

www.cbsnews.com

Click into the CBS News site and scroll down to podcasts. Locate *CBS Evening News* with Katie Couric Video Podcasts, and you will find a December 9, 2008, interview with Howard Schultz, head of Starbucks. In "Eye To Eye: Coffee Talk," Couric speaks with Schultz about the depressed economy's effect on his company. Schultz highlights a recent study, citing that consumers' level of trust and confidence in the Starbucks brand is at an all-time high—nearly 86 percent. For more than 30 years, he explains, the company has achieved a balance between profitability and social responsibility. Customers want to support businesses that have values similar to their own, and he expects Starbucks to be stronger once the world emerges from the present downturn. Schultz serves up a long-term approach to success and survival. "Success is not an entitlement. You have to earn it, and Starbucks is no different," the CEO summarizes. This is 4 minutes and 53 seconds of coffee chat at its best.

Continue on for another session of coffee chatter on December 9, 2008 with "Trouble Brewing at Starbucks," as Schultz and Couric visit again and discuss the future of Starbucks. Starbucks' sales had dropped 9 percent since the end of September, and Couric asks some hard-hitting questions about survival in the down economy. The recent decline is the company's largest in 37 years. Watch as Schultz candidly recounts his plans to weather the current economic bumps. Schultz believes he can save the company $400 million a year, for example, by cutting transportation costs and reducing waste. Offering advice to entrepreneurs, he says, "Great opportunities have been created in tough economic times." It is a highly straightforward discussion you won't want to miss.

Acronyms

BMI—Body mass index
C-N—Carbon-Nitrogen
C.A.F.E.—Coffee and Farmer Equity (in Starbucks' C.A.F.E. Practices)
CAT—Classroom assistance time
CEO—Chief executive officer
CI—Conservation International
CQI—Coffee Quality Institute
CSR—Corporate social responsibility
DJIA—Dow Jones Industrial Average
EMEA—Europe, Middle East, Africa
EPA—Environmental Protection Agency
EPS—Earnings per share
FAO—Food and Agriculture Organization of the United Nations
FLO—Fairtrade Labelling Organizations International
FY—Fiscal year
GAAP—Generally accepted accounting principles
GDP—Gross Domestic Product
GMOs—Genetically modified organisms
GS—Global Select
ICE—Intercontinental Exchange
ICO—International Coffee Organization
ICS—Institute for Coffee Studies
IPO—Initial public offering
IWW—Industrial Workers of the World
LEED—Leadership in Energy and Environmental Design green building
  rating system

NASDAQ—National Association Securities Dealers Automated Quotations (an electronic stock exchange)

NBER—National Bureau of Economic Research

NCA—National Coffee Association

NLRB—National Labor Relations Board

P/E—Price-to-earnings ratio

PCF—Post-consumer recycled fiber

PET—Polyethylene terephthalate (plastic packaging material)

SBUX—Starbucks Corporation common stock

SCAA—Specialty Coffee Association of America

SWU—Starbucks Workers Union

TTM—Trailing 12 months

USAID—U.S. Agency for International Development

USD—U.S. dollars

USDA—U.S. Department of Agriculture

USGBC—U.S. Green Building Council

Wi-Fi—Wireless fidelity

WTO—World Trade Organization

Bibliography

"100 Best Companies to Work for 2008." *Fortune*, January 22, 2008. Available at www.money.cnn.com/magazines/fortune (Rankings) from the February 4, 2008, issue (accessed October 26, 2008).

About Starbucks Union. Starbucks Workers Union. Available at www.starbuck sunion.org (accessed January 17, 2009).

About Us. Dunkin' Donuts. Available at www.dunkindonuts.com (accessed February 19, 2009).

Adamy, J. "McDonald's Coffee Strategy is Tough to Sell." *Wall Street Journal*, October 27, 2008. Available at www.online.wsj.com (accessed January 2, 2009).

———. "Starbucks Tests $1 Cup of Coffee, Free Refills." *Wall Street Journal*, January 23, 2008. Available at www.online.wsj.com (accessed January 2, 2009).

Allison, M. "As Stores Close Starbucks Buys a Jet." *Seattle Times*, January 8, 2009. Available at www.seattletimes.nwsource.com (accessed March 10, 2009).

———. "Starbucks Trying to Sell its New Jet." *Seattle Times*, January 28, 2009. Available at www.seattletimes.nwsource.com (accessed March 10, 2009).

———. "Starbucks Puts Third Corporate Jet Up for Sale." *Seattle Times*, March 6, 2009. Available at www.seattletimes.nwsource.com (accessed March 10, 2009).

———. "Starbucks Thrives in China, Attacked in Beirut, London." *Seattle Times*, January 14, 2006. Available at www.seattletimes.nwsource.com (accessed March 16, 2009).

———. "Seattle's Best Coffee Puts Out Call for Franchisees." *Seattle Times*, February 10, 2009. Available at www.seattletimes.nwsource.com (accessed March 9, 2009).

———. "Starbucks Steps Up Coffee Bean Sales in Europe." *Seattle Times*, March 5, 2009. Available at www.seattletimes.nwsource.com (accessed March 13, 2009).

———. "Starbucks Sued over Unchecked Ambition." *Seattle Times*, September 26, 2006. Available at www.seattletimes.nwsource.com (accessed January 7, 2009).

Anderson. R. "Starbucks Antitrust Lawsuit Settled." *Daily Weekly*, May 30, 2008. Available at www.blogs.seattleweekly.com/dailyweekly/ (accessed January 7, 2009).

Andrejczak, M. "Starbucks CEO Seeks to Dispel 'Excess' Myth." *MarketWatch*, March 18, 2009. Available at www.marketwatch.com (accessed April 10, 2009).

Behar, H., and J. Goldstein. *It's Not about the Coffee: Leadership Principles from a Life at Starbucks*. New York: Penguin Group, 2007.

Boeing: Higher, Faster, Farther: 1970–1996. Boeing. Available at www.boeing.com (accessed September 7, 2008).

"BofA to Sell 3 Corporate Jets, Helicopter." Associated Press Charlotte (AP) *News & Record*, February 4, 2009. Available at www.news-record.com (accessed March 13, 2009).

Bottled Water. National Resource Defense Council. Reviewed March, 25, 2008. Available at www.nrdc.org (accessed January 19, 2009).

Bureau of Labor Statistics. *Occupational Outlook Handbook.* 2008–2009 Edition. Available at www.bls.gov (accessed December 31, 2008).

Business Cycle Dating Committee, National Bureau of Economic Research. *Determination of the December 2007 Peak in Economic Activity.* December 11, 2008. Available at www.nber.org (accessed January 20, 2009).

Business Digest. "Starbucks Roasting Plant to be Built in South Carolina." *Seattle Times*, April 10, 2007. Available at http://seattletimes.nwsource.com (accessed March 8, 2009).

Buzby, J., and S. Haley. *Amber Waves.* June 2007. Available at www.ers.usda.gov (accessed August 12, 2008).

Capuchin Franciscan Frequently Asked Questions. The Capuchin Franciscans. Available at www.beafriar.com (accessed January 12, 3009).

"CEO Compensation: Lists." *Forbes*, April 30, 2008. Available at www.forbes.com (accessed November 4, 2008).

"Citigroup Nixes Plan to Buy $50M Corporate Jet." *Fox News*, January 27, 2009. Available at www.foxnews.com (accessed March 13, 2009).

Clark, T. *A Double Tall Tale of Caffeine, Commerce, and Culture.* New York: Little, Brown and Company, 2007.

Coffee. National Geographic, 1999. Available at www.nationalgeographic.com (accessed August 15, 2008).

Company Fact Sheet: Starbucks Coffee Company. Starbucks Coffee Company, February 2008. Available at www.starbucks.com (accessed October 14, 2008).

Company Information. Caribou Coffee Company, Inc. Available at www.cariboucoffee.com (accessed February 19, 2009).

Company Information. Peet's Coffee & Tea. Available at www.peets.com (accessed February 19, 2009).

Company Profile. Starbucks Coffee Company, February 2008. Available at www.starbucks.com (accessed October 26, 2008).

Corporate McDonald's. McDonald's Corporation. Available at www.mcdonalds.com (accessed February 19, 2009).

EthosWater: Helping Children Get Clean Water. EthosWater, c/o Starbucks Coffee Company. Available at www.ethoswater.com (accessed January 15, 2009).

Fact Sheet: Starbucks Partners and Unions. Starbucks Coffee Company, August 8, 2006. Available at www.starbucks.com (accessed January 17, 2009).

Fellner, K. *Wrestling with Starbucks: Conscience, Capital, and Cappuccino.* New Brunswick, NJ: Rutgers University Press, 2008.

Fitzgerald, E. "Starbucks Buys Hear Music Chain." *Billboard*, December 4, 1999. Available at www.allbusiness.com (accessed February 9, 2009).

Greater China: Starbucks Coffee International. Starbucks Newsroom, available at www.news.starbucks.com (accessed June 8, 2009).

H. D. "Boot Camp Brewhaha." *Training*, July 17, 2004. Available at www.allbusiness.com (accessed October 25, 2008).

Harris, J. "Ethics in a Bottle." *Fortune Small Business*, November 5, 2007. Available at www.moneycnn.com (accessed January 15, 2009).

Herbst, M. "Starbucks' Union Blues." *Business Week*, December 31, 2008. Available at www.businessweek.com (accessed January 17, 2009).

Hewitt, R., Jr. *Coffee: Its History, Cultivation, and Uses.* New York: D. Appleton and Company, 1872. rpt. University of Michigan University Library.

History of Coffee. Starbucks Coffee Company, 2008. Available at www.starbucks.com (accessed August 15, 2008).

History & Chronology: Fact Sheet 2. Lloyd's of London. Available at www.lloyds.com (accessed August 18, 2008).

Hubbard, R. G., and A. P. O'Brien. *Microeconomics*, 2nd Edition. Upper Saddle River, NJ: Pearson Prentice Hall, 2008.

James, A. "Starbucks Won't Slug It Out in Ad Wars." *Seattle Post-Intelligencer*, December 10, 2008. Available at www.seattlepi.com (accessed January 4, 2009).

———. "Starbucks Newest Item is Hot, Chocolaty." *Seattle Post-Intelligencer*, September 28, 2008. Available at www.seattlepi.com (accessed March 10, 2009).

———. "6,700 Starbucks Jobs at Risk." *Seattle Post-Intelligencer*, January 29, 2009. Available at www.seattlepi.com (accessed March 1, 2009).

Logren, S. "Coffee-Based Log Burns Cleaner-But No Starbucks Smell." National Geographic News, October 25, 2004. Available at www.news.nationalgeographic.com/news (accessed June 12, 2009).

McDermott, T. "Cash Crop." *Seattle Times*, November 28, 1993. Available at www.seattletimes.nwsource.com (accessed August 23, 2008).

Michelli, J. *The Starbucks Experience: 5 Principles for Turning Ordinary into Extraordinary.* New York: McGraw-Hill, 2007.

Moore, J. *Tribal Knowledge: Business Wisdom Brewed from the Grounds of Starbucks Corporate Culture.* Chicago: Kaplan Publishing, 2006.

Mulady, K. "Retail Notebook: As Starbucks Marks 30th Year, a Look Back at Beginning." *Seattle Post-Intelligencer*, September 8, 2001. Available at www.seattlepi.com (accessed August 23, 2008).

News Release. "Caribou Coffee Gives Decaf Drinkers a Needed Boost." Caribou Coffee Company, Inc., January 29, 2009. Available at www.cariboucoffee.com Investors (accessed February 24, 2009).

News Release. "Foreclosure Activity Increases 81 Percent in 2008." RealtyTrac, January 15, 2009. Available at www.realtytrac.org (accessed January 20, 2009).

News Release. "Great Start for Great Teachers." Starbucks Coffee Company, September 4, 2008. Available at www.starbucks.com (accessed January 21, 2009).

News Release. "Howard Schultz Transformation Agenda Communication #3." Starbucks Coffee Company, January 30, 2008. Available at www.starbucks.com (accessed January 1, 2009).

News Release. "New CDC Study Finds No Increase in Obesity among Adults; But Levels Still High." CDC National Center for Health Statistics Office of Communication, November 28, 2007. Available at www.cdc.gov (accessed November 30, 2008).

News Release. "New Starbucks Chocolates Debuts: Blending Premium Artisan-Style Chocolate with Authentic Coffeehouse Flavors." Starbucks Coffee Company, March 4, 2008. Available at www.starbucks.com (accessed March 10, 2009).

News Release. "New Starbucks Signature Hot Chocolate Debuts: Intensifying the Chocolate Experience with Gourmet Flavors." Starbucks Coffee Company, September 30, 2008. Available at www.starbucks.com (accessed March 10, 2009).

News Release. "Peet's Coffee & Tea, Inc. Reports 26% Increase in Fourth Quarter 2008 Diluted Earnings Per Share and Reports Fiscal Year 2008 Results." Peet's Coffee & Tea, Inc., February 12, 2009. Available at www.peets.com (accessed February 27, 2009).

News Release. "Seattle's Best Coffee Expands Franchising Program in U.S." Seattle's Best Coffee, February 3, 2009. Available at www.seattlesbest.com (accessed March 9, 2009).

News Release. "Signature Starbucks Beverages Inspire New Super-Premium Ice Cream Line." Starbucks Coffee Company, March 24, 2009. Available at www. news.starbucks.com (accessed April 10, 2009).

News Release. "Starbucks and Kraft Foods Expand European Distribution of Packaged Starbucks Coffee to Consumers in France and Germany." Starbucks Coffee Company, March 5, 2009. Available at www.news.starbucks.com (accessed March 13, 2009).

News Release. "Starbucks and (RED) Debut the (STARBUCKS)RED Card to Help Save Lives in Africa." Starbucks Coffee Company, December 18, 2008. Available at www.starbucks.com (accessed February 24, 2009).

News Release. "Starbucks Appoints Olden Lee as Interim Executive Vice President, Partner Resources." Starbucks Coffee Company, April 6, 2009. Available at www.news.starbucks.com (accessed April 9, 2009).

News Release. "Starbucks Details Strategy for Profitable Growth." Starbucks Coffee Company, March 18, 2009. Available at www.news.starbucks.com (accessed April 10, 2009).

New Release. "Starbucks Extends Health & Wellness Offerings with Five New Healthy Breakfast Options." Starbucks Coffee Company, September 3, 2008. Available at www.starbucks.com (accessed December 5, 2008).

News Release. "Starbucks John Culver to Succeed Gerado Lopez as Executive Vice President; President, Global Consumer Products, Foodservice and Seattle's Best Coffee." Starbucks Coffee Company, February 9, 2009. Available at www. starbucks.com (accessed February 11, 2009).

News Release. "Starbucks Joins Call for National Service and Asks, 'Are You In?'" Starbucks Coffee Company, January 14, 2009. Available at www.starbucks.com (accessed February 11, 2009).

News Release. "Starbucks Opens LEED Certified Coffee Roasting Plant." Starbucks Coffee Company, February 19, 2009. Available at www.starbucks.com (accessed March 8, 2009).

News Release. "Starbucks Reports First Quarter Fiscal 2009 Results." Starbucks Coffee Company, January 28, 2009. Available at www.starbucks.com (accessed March 1, 2009).

News Release. "Starbucks Reports Fourth Quarter and Fiscal 2008 Results." Starbucks Coffee Company, November 10, 2008. Available at www.starbucks.com (accessed December 27, 2008).

News Release. "Starbucks Statement: Hot Beverage Cups and Recycling." Starbucks Coffee Company, September 18, 2007. Available at www.starbucks.com (accessed January 5, 2009).

News Release. "Starbucks Unveils New Strategic Initiatives to Transform and Innovate the Customer Experience." Starbucks Coffee Company, March 19, 2008. Available at www.starbucks.com (accessed December 10, 2008; February 16, 2009).

News Release. "Starbucks VIA Ready Brew: A Breakthrough in Instant Coffee." Starbucks Coffee Company, February 17, 2009. Available at www.starbucks.com (accessed March 2, 2009).

News Release. "Steeped in Coffeehouse Tradition, Starbucks Introduces New Hand-crafted Tea Beverages and Encourages Customers to Take a Much Needed Break." Starbucks Coffee Company, December 30, 2008. Available at www.starbucks.com (accessed March 1, 2009).

News Release. "When Coffee Dreams, It Dreams of Chocolate: Starbucks Coffee Company's Global Consumer Products Group and The Hershey Company Announce Agreement to Launch Premium Chocolate Platform." Starbucks Coffee Company and The Hershey Company, July 19, 2007. Available at www.thehersheycompany.com (accessed March 10, 2009).

News Release. "Winner in the Battle of the Brews: Dunkin' Donuts Beat Starbucks in Independent Nationwide Taste Test." Dunkin' Donuts, October 30, 2008. Available at www.dunkindonuts.com (accessed January 3, 2009).

New York Board of Trade. *Coffee: Futures and Options.* New York: New York Board of Trade, 2004.

Nutrition by the Cup: Drink options to fit the way you live. Starbucks Coffee Company, 2007. Available at starbucks.com/nutrition (accessed June 8, 2009).

P-I Staff. "Seattle's Starbucks Center Earns National Green Certification." *Seattle Post-Intelligencer,* November 1, 2007. Available at www.seattlepi.com (accessed March 8, 2009).

"People of the Year 95: Gerald Baldwin, Peet's Coffee & Tea." *Tea & Coffee Trade Journal,* December 1, 1995. Available at www.allbusiness.com (accessed September 8, 2008).

Phillips, N. "Starbucks Plant Has Its Perks: Employees, Calhoun County Leaders Value Roasting Facility." *The State,* February 20, 2009. Available at www.thestate.com (accessed March 8, 2009).

Ramsland, K. *The Starbucks Shooter.* TruTV, Turner Broadcasting System, Inc. Available at www.trutv.com (accessed December 30, 2008).

Ross, B., and C. Herman. "GM, Ford Will Sell Corporate Jet Fleet." *ABC News,* December 2, 2008. Available at www.abcnewsgo.com (accessed March 13, 2009).

Sanderson, H. "China-Grown Coffee Launched: Starbucks Says It's 'Barely Scratching the Surface.'" The Associated Press (Beijing), *Seattle Post-Intelligencer,* January 14, 2009. Available at www.seattlepi.com (accessed March 16, 2009).

Schiller, B. R. *The Micro Economy Today,* 11th edition. New York: McGraw-Hill Irwin, 2008.

Schultz, H., and D. Jones Yang. *Pour Your Heart into It: How Starbucks Built a Company One Cup at a Time.* New York: Hyperion, 1997.

Simmons, J. *My Sister's a Barista: How They Made Starbucks a Home Away from Home.* London: Cyan Books, 2005.

Sniegowski, D. "Seattle's Best Coffee Stirs up Coffee Wars by Franchising." *Blue MauMau,* February 5, 2009. Available at www.bluemaumau.org (accessed March 9, 2009).

————. "Interview: Franchising Seattle's Best Coffee." *Blue MauMau,* February 6, 2009. Available at www.bluemaumau.org (accessed March 9, 2009).

Specialty Coffee Association of America Fact Sheet: Specialty Coffee Facts. Specialty Coffee Association of America. Available at www.scaa.org (accessed January 8, 2009).

Specialty Coffee Association of America Fact Sheet: Specialty Coffee Retail in the U.S.A. 2006. Specialty Coffee Association of America. Available at www.scaa.org (accessed January 8, 2009).

Starbucks China. Starbucks Corporation. Available at www.starbucks.com.cn (accessed June 9, 2009).

Starbucks Coffee Company 02-CA-37548. The National Labor Relations Board Division of Judges New York Branch Office. Mindy E. Landow; December 19, 2008.

Starbucks Corporation Board of Directors: Brief Bios. Starbucks Coffee Company. Revised March 19, 2008. Available at www.starbucks.com (accessed February 9, 2009).

Starbucks Corporation: Corporate Governance Principles and Practices for the Board of Directors. Starbucks Coffee Company. Revised May 6, 2008. Available at www.starbucks.com (accessed January 20, 2009).

Starbucks Corporation: Corporate Social Responsibility Fiscal 2007 Annual Report. Starbucks Coffee Company. Available at www.starbucks.com (accessed November 20, 2008).

Starbucks Corporation: Fiscal 2007 Year in Review. Starbucks Coffee Company. Available at www.starbucks.com (accessed August 12, 2008).

Starbucks Corporation Form 8-K, filed February 9, 2009. United States Securities and Exchange Commission, Washington, DC.

Starbucks Corporation Form 10-K, filed November 24, 2008. United States Securities and Exchange Commission, Washington, DC.

Starbucks Corporation Form 10-K, filed February 4, 2009. United States Securities and Exchange Commission, Washington, DC.

"Store Wars: Cappuccino Kings." *BBC News,* June 9, 2004. Available at www.news.bbc.co.uk (accessed January 10, 2009).

Sullivan, P. "Alfred Peet; Put Buzz in Gourmet Coffee." *Washington Post,* September 1, 2007. Available at www.washingtonpost.com (accessed January 1, 2009).

The Story of Coffee. International Coffee Organization. Available at www.ico.org (accessed August 14, 2008).

The World Factbook. Central Intelligence Agency. Available at www.cia.gov (accessed June 9, 2009).

Toops, D. "Starbuck's David Olsen: Awakening a Passion for Coffee." *Food Processing,* August 1, 1996. Available at www.allbusiness.com (accessed October 10, 2008).

Wild, A. *Coffee: A Dark History.* New York: W.W. Norton & Company, Inc., 2004.

Williams, D. "Boston Tea Party." *The Encyclopedia Americana.* International ed. Danbury, CT: Grolier Incorporated, 2004.

Personal Interviews

Barrow, Katie (public relations manager, TransFair USA), interview by author, November 13, 2008.

Berenbach, Shari (president and CEO, Calvert Foundation), interview by author, November 10, 2008.

Cleveland, James (president, Jumpstart), interview by author, November 21, 2008.

Lingle, Ted (executive director, Coffee Quality Institute), interview by author, November 26, 2008.

Spokesperson for ICE Futures U.S., interview by author, October 31, 2008.

Index